Student Success Secrets

 By Eric Jensen

 Fifth Edition

 Illustrated by Tom Kerr

BARRON'S

"There are no limitations to the self. There are no limitations to its potential. You can adopt artificial limitations through ignorance."

Jane Roberts

All inquiries should be addressed to:
Barron's Educational Series, Inc.
250 Wireless Boulevard
Hauppauge, New York 11788
http://www.barronseduc.com

Library of Congress Catalog Card No. 2002040773

ISBN-13: 978-0-7641-2007-7
ISBN-10: 0-7641-2007-7

Library of Congress Cataloging-in-Publicaton Data
Jensen, Eric.
    Student success secrets / by Eric Jensen ; illustrated by Tom Kerr.
— 5th ed.
      p. cm.
    Summary: Provides easy-to-follow guidelines for succeeding in
school and beyond, including note-taking, study methods, test-taking,
and resources for papers, and vocabulary building.
    Includes bibliographical references (p.).
    ISBN 0-7641-2007-7
    1. Study skills—Juvenile literature.   2. Report writing—Juvenile
literature.   3. Reading comprehension—Juvenile literature.   4. Notetaking—Juvenile literature. [1. Study skills.   2. Report writing.
3. Reading comprehension.   4. Note-taking.] I. Title.

LB1049 .J43   2003
371.3'028'1—dc21   2002040773

PRINTED IN THE UNITED STATES OF AMERICA
19 18 17 16 15 14 13 12 11 10

TABLE OF CONTENTS

PREFACE

This book is about learning and succeeding. If you combine motivation, perseverance, and effective learning strategies, you're on the right path. I discovered this in a roundabout way. As a student, it seemed that the only classes I did well in were those in which I liked either the subject or the teacher. I never really thought about how to learn and how to apply that learning to school. But the better I got at learning *how* to learn, the easier and more fun school became. By the time I got to graduate school, it was a lot of fun, but I missed out on a lot of learning and fun along the way.

Years later, it turned out that my specialty was understanding the brain and how we learn. Right now, I study from the scientists who research the brain and the learning process. No one ever taught me much brain information when I was in school, but I sure am using it now. I can be considered a lifelong learner. That's pretty important. In fact, the greatest single competitive advantage anyone can have is the ability to learn. Specialties, jobs, careers, and even industries can go out-of-date or out of business. But if you can learn new skills and new information quickly, you'll always be in demand, either as an employee or as a businessperson. Reassuring thought, isn't it?

ACKNOWLEDGMENTS

I offer a heartfelt thank you to all the students who came to me with open minds. Each and every one gave me the opportunity to do what I like to do the most—to help others succeed. To those who believed in me, and most of all, in themselves, thank you! I appreciate the confidence I have gained from many supporters and friends. These include my parents, my students, my teachers, and my wife. I also thank Barron's Educational Series, Inc., and the editors who have worked with me over the years to make this project happen.

INTRODUCTION

Everyone likes to be successful. Yet, success is not getting A's in school, being popular, getting a scholarship, or making money. Although others may try to convince you that success is a new car or good work hours, these accomplishments are only the immediate rewards. Long-term success is a journey. There is no destination for that magic we all call success. It's a continual gut-level feeling of confidence that you are on the right path. It is a powerful state of mind wherein the world is yours for the asking.

The unhappiest person is the person without choices. To acquire more choices, you need assets. Education can be a definite asset, whether formal or informal. It can open up many doors that were previously closed, so get the best education you can. Even if you don't use the academic information, you may use the contacts you make in school later on in life.

If you decide that college is the right path for you, then try to go to the best school you can afford. It may help you get a better education and have an opportunity to associate with more successful students and staff. In addition, your school's reputation will be carried with you for years. Once you have chosen your school, do the very best you can. Success is an important habit to establish—good habits formed in school will be with you throughout your life.

In this book, you will become familiar with various learning strategies and be shown how some of these techniques can be applied to school success. You will be provided with simple, effective, and dynamic tools to use every day, as you must do to succeed. This book is based on my own research and years of experience. It conveys the enthusiasm and attitudes that have been proven successful time and again. It includes important information you need to know to become a successful student. I have enjoyed writing this book and I hope that you will enjoy reading it.

The best way to read this book is to follow these three steps:

1. Browse through the whole book. Simply turn all the pages and scan them with a light-hearted look at each page. Do that before you give any page a more detailed reading.

2. Wherever you decide to start reading, take notes. Use colored pens and doodle as you read. Make sense out of it;

draw pictures or write out key ideas. As you stay active while you read, your concentration and comprehension stay up, too.

3. Turn your favorite ideas into key phrases on 3" × 5" cards, or make a colorful poster reminder. That way, the ideas you like the most can stay alive for you and keep giving you value for years.

Good luck!

1

MOTIVATION:
How to Tap Your Inner Genius

Welcome to the world of student success. If you're ready to succeed in school, you're in the right place. If you're ready to learn to read better, read faster, study more efficiently, and stay focused, keep reading—you're on the right path. But, what if you have tried to reach these goals before, but couldn't seem to maintain your motivation long enough to accomplish them? What do you do about that? There is an answer. And you may be surprised to learn where you'll find it.

The secret of motivation is between your ears. That's right; it's your brain. Surprisingly, your brain is far more capable than you might think. Although it weighs just three pounds, it consumes about 25 percent of your body's energy. It's storage capacity seems almost unlimited. It has about 100 billion cells that can communicate with each other, making the potential connections for learning far into the trillions! (That's enough for any class you'll be taking!)

So, if your brain is so awesome, why has it been tough to get motivated in the past, you might ask. The answer is simple. You could have the most high-powered computer, car, or rocket on the planet, but if you don't know *how* to use it, it would certainly be frustrating, wouldn't it? Well, your brain is that way. It's a complex electrochemical system, and when you're motivated, it's because you have just the right chemical balance. That means dopamine, norepinephrine, and serotonin. That's what neurochemicals do—they get you ready to go. It isn't necessary for you to buy products that boost these neurochemicals (unless your doctor finds that there is a medical need for them). Too much of each one can produce negative side effects. Therefore, it's helpful to rely on your body's natural method of producing these neurochemicals. Fortunately, it's good at it. You just need to know how.

In spite of how much potential our brain offers each and every one of us, we were never given an owner's manual, a how-to book on the best way to use it. That's kind of what this book will discuss. It's a combination of some insights about how your brain works, and some useful strategies for school success. Let's start with the basics. How on earth do we get ourselves motivated to even begin school success?

W-I-I-F-M? WHAT'S IN IT FOR ME?

Before we go any further, let's settle something. Who says that getting high grades is all that good? Is there really much of an advantage in being a terrific student? Some students say yes. Here's their argument:

The Benefits of Successful Study Habits

- Better studying takes less time. That gives you more time for other things.

- Your self-image improves. You might find that you feel better about yourself, and this confidence can transfer to other things.

- You may gain better comprehension. This could lead to a better understanding of the world around you, which makes life much more interesting.

- You'll experience less frustration and rereading. That makes things much more fun.

- You can expect better grades. That's likely to lead to more self-confidence and more choices in life.

- If you get better grades, your chances for scholarships increase. That means you can get your college education partly or fully paid, allowing you to fully enjoy the college experience, instead of having to work part-time.

- Getting better grades means you can play the school game well. If you can do that, you'll probably be able to master the working world better, too.

- You might gain much more knowledge. Knowledge is power; the more you know, the more choices you have.

- Your success can lead to greater confidence in academic and social situations, instead of embarrassment.

- Better learning success can also sharpen thinking habits. This means you may be able to make better decisions, ones that save you grief and make your life more interesting.

On the other hand, there's not much to be gained by doing poorly in school. You could collect some sympathy from those who feel sorry for you. Or, you could get others to expect so little of you that they leave you alone and stop asking you what you are going to do with your life. But aside from that, there aren't many benefits to having academic difficulties. Life, as you know, holds so many possibilities. In fact, it's a good idea to start with figuring out exactly what you *do* want. You might already have done this. It's simply called **goal-setting.**

YOUR MIND NATURALLY SEEKS GOALS

First, what's the difference between your brain and your mind? You may have said before, "I'm going out of my mind!" But you wouldn't say, "I'm going out of my brain." Your brain is the soft, mushy, three-pound pink tissue inside your head. It has its own wired-in biological impulses. For instance, it thrives on oxygen, glucose, and amino acids. Not very romantic! Now your mind, that's simply the brain in action. It's the part of you that wants a hot fudge sundae, but then you say to yourself, "I'll get one after I study for this upcoming test." So you wait a while, and get it later. Get the difference?

Give your mind a goal and it wants to reach it. Your mind is very goal-directed. Imagine a goal with color, sound, taste, smell, and feel. Now your mind wants to reach that goal. If you make the goal more real, it wants it even more. Make the goal extra-attractive, and now the mind *really* wants it. Make the goal an absolute, definite *must have* and your mind really, really, *really* wants it.

So what does this have to do with school? It's easy. Set short-term goals. Set long-term goals. Set easy goals. Set hard goals. Set goals you want. Set goals you know are good for you. But set some goals!

Let's say you already have a specific goal in mind, such as a career in technology, writing, medicine, teaching, acting, or law. Now, you may need to make those goals more specific. It is not enough to say, "I want to be a scientist." You should decide what field you wish to study and when you plan to enter that field. You may change your mind later, but having clear goals now can help you to begin the journey toward attaining them.

Some people may caution you not to set unrealistic goals. Since you don't really know yet how much motivation and capacity you have, set both short-term and long-term goals. Set goals that you think you can achieve and goals that you dream of achieving. What's realistic? Do you know that a blind man climbed Mt. Everest, the tallest mountain in the world? Did you know that famous people with the reading disorder *dyslexia* include a Nobel Laureate, movie stars, wealthy executives, and inventors? Do you know that a ninety-year-old runner completed the 26-mile-long Boston marathon? How realistic were those goals? If you can dream, and are willing to commit to striving for your goals, you have a chance. Only later can you learn whether the goal was realistic or unrealistic.

Next, the time commitment is important. By setting a date for goal completion, you have created focus and purpose. Goals are great, not only because they help you stay on track, but also because they help keep you from being distracted by other paths that may sound interesting. The time deadline gets you focused on the *when* as much as the *what*.

Finally, give yourself reasons to reach your goals. Goals and time deadlines create a laser-sharp deadline, but a reason is the "fuel" for striving toward it. In sports, every team sets as their goal winning the championship, but only one team wins it. Is it always due to talent? Not really. It's usually the team that wants it more. The one that is more dedicated, more motivated to win, and more intense in emotion! That's right, your feelings are important. The stronger you feel about reaching your goals, the more likely you'll do it.

One more thing before you write down your goals. It's valuable not only to have strong reasons to reach your goals but also to feel a sense of loss if you don't. As an example, let's say you wanted to do well in a class; that's your goal. Why do well? It might help your grades and your self-confidence, and to feel satisfaction or to get a scholarship. That's the plus side. But the minus side is there, too.

If you *don't* get a good grade in that class, the opposite might happen: You could get discouraged, miss out on a scholarship, and learn very little. See what I mean? Everything has both an up and a down side to it.

By the way, are goals the whole answer? No, just a big part of it. Sometimes students set goals but don't reach them. If goals are so important for your mind, why doesn't it always work, you ask. Good question. The answer may surprise you.

HOW TO MAKE GOALS HAPPEN

There are specific ways to set goals that will make you more likely to reach them. That's what we'll talk about now.

Let's pretend for a moment that you are driving from Los Angeles to Boston. Would you take a different road than if you were going from Washington, D.C., to Chicago? Of course. What road or path you take depends on your final destination, not just where you'll be after ten minutes of driving. It's the same way in goal-setting. To figure out what to do today, you'll need to know where you'll want to be in 20 years. Unsure of or worried about the future? Relax. You'll have plenty of time to work out those details. For now, at least, start with the basics.

In your mind, go into the future, 20 years from now. You may not know what your career will be, but you do know you'll want certain things, such as an interesting job, a house, and family. But who knows? Maybe you'll want something different. What you dream of, you might get, so you might as well dream of something that is really satisfying. A job, a spouse, a family, a home? It's your life—go ahead and dream.

STOP AND TAKE ACTION

◆ Now, get a pen or pencil. Let's start with 20 years from now. What are your goals for then? Go ahead and fill in the lines below with ideas of things you might like to do, to have, or to have accomplished in 20 years.

Example: *Work in the computer industry, be married with one child, live in a warm climate, and be in great health.*

Figure out how old you'll be in 20 years. What kind of education do you want to have? Family, money, skills, lifestyle, expertise, etc. If you are unsure, it's okay to dream a bit. Nobody has a crystal ball, so it's all going to be *guesswork*. Put something down. It's better to strive forward with a goal you later change than to have no goal set at all. Take your time.

◆ Go ahead and fill in the lines above. Remember, you only *get* your goals if you *set* them first. Now, title the second section, **Five years.** What will you need to have accomplished in five years to be able to reach your 20-year goals?

Example: *I will be in college, getting good grades, being active, healthy, and having a great time.*

Where will you need to be in five years? In school? At work? Take a few moments and write out all your goals.

◆ Did you complete those lines above? If not, why not just give it a try? Now, go to the third section of your paper. You can tell that we are getting closer to the present moment. This section is titled **Six months.** In order to reach your five-year goals, what will you need to have accomplished in the next six months?

Example: *I will have taken a study skills course, I'll get my grades up to a B average, and I'll be working out three times a week.*

First, what month will it be six months from now? Write out all of the goals that you'd like to reach six months from today.

_____

_____

_____

◆ Finally, let's get our goals right out in front of us. You know what you want to do in 20 years, five years, and six months. Now, what will you need to be doing in the next week, to reach your six-month goals? Go ahead and figure it out.

Example: *This week, I'll check around school, in the yellow pages, or with teachers for a study skills or speed-reading course. I'll start doing something active this week (swimming, powerwalking, etc.). I'll also post my goals for this week, six months, five years, and 20 years.*

You see, today's actions lead to tomorrow's results. What happens in the future is not always in your control, but you do have a lot to do with it. Setting long-

and short-term goals is a way to influence the future. You are inventing your future just like a scientist invents a new gadget.

_____

_____

_____

◆ In the space below, write at least five reasons *why it is important* for you to reach your goals. (As an example: "I'll gain self-confidence, earn more money," etc.)

_____

_____

_____

◆ Now, write at least *three bad things that could happen to you* if you don't reach your goals. (As an example: "I'll feel bad about myself, I'll disappoint my parents, or I'll be poor.")

_____

_____

_____

HOW TO MAINTAIN FOCUS

Once your goals are set, keep them alive. Setting your goals doesn't mean there's nothing left to do. The ability to stay fixed and single-minded on a goal is the stuff dreams are made of. After envisioning and even planning a house, you still need to do the building and maintenance of it. In school, it's important to use your skills to focus, in the right way.

As an example:

> Melissa was a sophomore at James Madison High. She was really interested in a guy in her English class, but the more she thought about him, the worse her concentration became. She missed directions in class and homework assignments. Her constant daydreaming and infatuation got her in real trouble one day; she totally missed hearing about an upcoming test. As a result, she was unprepared and almost failed it. It was a tough way to learn a lesson.

There are plenty of distractions in school. How on earth can you stay focused and still have any kind of a life? Just how do you do it? The answer is: self-discipline.

STOP AND TAKE ACTION

◆ Take a minute out of your busy schedule to relax.

◆ Keep your four sets of goals real in your mind.

◆ Close your eyes and picture yourself strongly, vividly, and clearly reaching your goals. See this in great detail.

◆ Notice what you're wearing, what you're doing as you see yourself reaching them.

◆ Feel and hear yourself being successful, happy, and excited as you reach each and every goal in your imagination.

Practice this visualization every day, and the desire will build. It is important to reinforce your desire by reviewing your specific goal, a definite plan. Then fuel the dreams with the power of your constant and creative imagination. Remember, as long as you make your goal positive, real, attractive, and worth achieving, your mind will be naturally drawn to reach it.

USE YOUR BEST MIND

Have you ever said to yourself, "I don't know what I was thinking. I must have been out of my mind!" Many of us have done something that we regret later. When it comes to school and getting good grades, use your "best mind." That's the one that keeps asking questions until you get the quality of information you want. Questions send the mind in many directions, searching for possible answers. Asking questions and solving problems is actually the best exercise you can do for your brain. In fact, that's the equivalent of an aerobic workout for the brain.

How do you tap into your "best mind" for schoolwork? Find out what you are unsure of by asking questions until you're satisfied. Let's say there's a class in which you're having a tough time. Let's figure out what questions would be most useful to do better in the class. You might start with questions like these:

- What is the most important theme running throughout the course? (In a history class, the theme might be economic expansion drives civilization.)

- What stories, analogies, or metaphors could explain the key concepts? (In a biology class, a metaphor for the brain might be a rain forest.)

- What are the movies or videos that make this subject come alive? (In an English class, the movie *Shakespeare in Love* might be helpful.)

- What is it that, if I knew it, would help me understand other key concepts? You might want to ask the teacher to clarify the most relevant aspect of the topic for you.

- Could you make a topic map, or draw out the topic in key areas? (In math, you might create a flowchart that maps out the steps to solving a problem.)

- What are the most critical vocabulary words to know?

- Who can I go to in order to get additional help?

There are, of course, many other questions you can ask. For example, "What's going to be on the test?" is a popular one. One of the real skills in life is learning to ask the right questions. So, if one question fails to give you the information you want, keep asking. The information you want and need may be in the next one. Before questioning your teacher or others, however, ask yourself if you might actually already know the answer. Sometimes, out of insecurity or uncertainty, we assume that others have answers that we do not know.

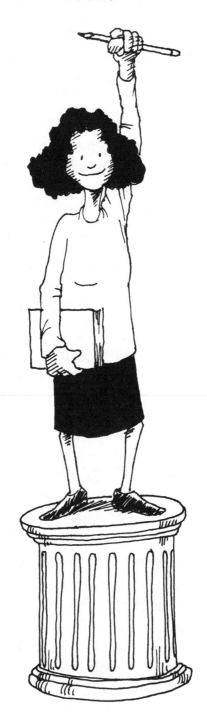

STOP AND
TAKE ACTION

◆ Make a list of questions that you would like to ask of your teacher. Maybe another list for your parents. Maybe a list for another student you might study with.

◆ Before you ask them the questions, ask an even more important one: "I have a few questions; is this a good time to ask them?" If it's not a good time, find out when a good time would be to ask them.

◆ Remember, information is power, knowledge is power, and if you don't know what you need to know, ask.

HOW TO DEVELOP
A WINNING ATTITUDE

Winning attitudes mean you expect to succeed. Your positive personality traits include attitudes, actions, and opinions. A winning attitude attracts other positive people, thus leading to mutual support and inspiration. A winning attitude means you're enthusiastic about life, you work on a healthy self-image, and make decisions promptly. You've seen others with that personality magic or some kind of charisma. How do they develop it? It's not hard, but it does take some time. Why? Everything you think has the possibility of leading to an action. Every action you take can lead to habit. Every habit you develop becomes part of your character and may contribute to a winning (or losing) attitude. So, it's easy to see that it all starts with your thoughts and simple actions. After all, they are the seeds you sow that become your habits and, eventually, your character. Let's start with some simple things.

STOP AND
TAKE ACTION

◆ **Believe in yourself.** Believe that you can and will succeed in school. You can probably think of many positive qualities about yourself (you are motivated enough to read this book, you are interested in school success, you have goals, etc.). Name three reasons you believe in yourself:

_____

_____

_____

◆ **Identify your support.** Why will you succeed? Because you have the resources to back yourself up if you are having a tough time. Your resources are everywhere (friends, parents, teachers, relatives, your home, a library, or media center, etc.). Name some of your own resources:

_____

_____

_____

◆ **Have a healthy mind and body.** A winning attitude goes well with a healthy mind and body. You've heard it all before: Eat lightly. Eat the proper balance of health-giving, wholesome foods. Exercise regularly and learn proper posture. Take care of your hair, teeth, nails, and complexion. Hold your head high and smile. Now, what can and will you do to be at your best and project that winning attitude? Name three things:

_____

_____

_____

◆ **Have the attitude of a winner.** A winning attitude means not that you *win* at everything, but that you have the *attitude* of a winner. Two teams play a football game. One wins and one loses. The winner is, however, not always the highest scorer. You may be surprised. If a team practices hard all week, they believe they can and will win. They play their hearts out, play fair, but lose the game. They have a winning attitude. If another team believes they deserve to win because they think they are superior people and the opposition team is made up of lowlifes—they cheat and play dirty, and still score more points—they are losers. The scoreboard says "winner" but you know who won in the real game of life. So, let's cut to the chase and get this straight: It's not what happens to you; it's how you deal with it. Name three bad things that have happened to you in the last few weeks (a low grade, a friend who hurt your feelings, or missing out on something important to you). Then name a positive, winning way for you to deal with that event.

Event   **Positive Ways to Deal with It**

_____

_____

_____

WHY CHOOSE FRIENDS CAREFULLY

We rarely think about some of the strongest influences on our lives. The people you see the most often affect you the most. People tend to have a general lifestyle that is similar to that of their friends. An important implication is that you may want to choose your friends carefully because, in doing so, you choose your future. By associating with those people who are your own role models, you are most apt to make some pleasant changes in yourself. So if your friends are considerate of others, healthy, happy, and well-rounded, then you are likely to acquire those traits also. Or, if your friends are high achievers who enter science or hobby fairs, become involved in athletics, drama, singing, or good jobs, you'll feel those influences, too.

Naturally, the opposite is also true. The old saying, "Birds of a feather flock together," has been proven accurate. You may acquire some poor habits if your friends are unsupportive, act tough, abuse drugs, drift without goals, or are in legal trouble. These so-called friends can set you back years by leading you away from your own goals. Friends who care about you, friends who tell the truth, friends who you can talk to—they are important. Everyone needs good-quality friends, and only by being a positive, happy person will you attract good friends.

As an example:

At Albert Einstein Middle School, Jim was mischievous and often destructive. One day, Jim and his two best friends were at a construction site where earth-moving vehicles were parked for the weekend. Because they disliked the fact that their neighborhood was being affected by new building, they decided to vandalize a bulldozer. When Jim put sand in the gas tank, his other friends felt uncomfortable, but they did nothing to stop the damage. On Monday, the police arrived and tracked down who did it. The parents were notified and the boys were arrested. Over time, Jim's two friends began to hang around him less and less. They learned that there's a difference between adventure and trouble.

Honesty is the cornerstone of your character, because it is the advertisement of your values. By being honest, you'll avoid embarrassing problems, such as having to cover one lie with another—or, worse yet, being confronted with the truth later on. Many of us have told little "white lies" at times, such as when we take credit for something that we really didn't deserve. However, we need to always ask ourselves why the lie is needed and think about the possible outcome.

Good friendship requires trust. Although most good friends will stick with you through good times and bad, if you are dishonest with them, you risk losing their friendship. In the same vein, if a friendship is not a positive experience for you and much of the time you have disagreements with the friend, you may need to make some changes. Either spend less time with that friend, or figure out how to get along better.

Whatever his or her needs, this friend does not have the right to ruin your happiness or your chances of reaching your goal. A good schoolmate can be a dynamic source of inspiration, knowledge, and enjoyment. By choosing positive, growing friends, you will find the path much easier. But, most agree, it is necessary to choose your friends carefully.

STOP AND TAKE ACTION

◆ Write out your three best friends' names. Next to their names, write out their strengths. What do you like most about them?

_____

_____

_____

◆ Now write out what you don't like about them. Are these negative qualities trivial or are they important to you?

_____

_____

_____

◆ Do you need to make any changes? If so, what will you do? When will you do it?

_____

_____

_____

HOW TO BUILD FAITH IN YOURSELF

Which comes first, success or having faith in yourself? Both are critical! One helps build the other. If you don't believe in yourself, there's no point in trying, is there? "If you think you're beaten, you are," means those without faith in themselves will surely fail. If you think you could use an occasional miracle in school, faith is especially important. Faith seems to be the basis of all miracles (couldn't everyone use a miracle now and then?) and the basis for all success. What builds faith? It's a positive attitude about two things—a belief in yourself and a belief in a higher power. You believe that you'll do the right thing at the right time. And, you believe that whatever happens is for the best anyway. If you think faith is a bunch of positive-thinking baloney, you'll enjoy this true story.

As an example:

Diane was in a car accident during her last year in Sharpstown High School. Doctors said she might never walk again. They didn't believe in her, but she very much believed in herself. First she was in a wheelchair; then she "graduated" to crutches. She worked her body hard, but any hopes of a decent social life in school were dashed. In spite of her natural beauty, she was ignored by guys—they figured, "Who wants a cripple?" By the time she finished college at the University of Houston, she was off crutches and her limp was gone. In time, she regained total health. Today, in her forties, she works out daily. She's been on strenuous mountain climbs, and enjoys perfect health.

The author should know the story above quite well; he married Diane! It's pretty amazing what humans have used their incredible willpower, belief, and faith to accomplish—to climb the Himalayas, slow their own heartbeat, and walk on hot coals, to name a few feats. So it can certainly be used more effectively to get A's and B's in school.

Maybe you've been thinking that you need that something extra to succeed. Do you think you lack tools, resources, opportunity, creativity, or intelligence? Forget that negative thinking. You have not been short-changed! Let's take inventory to find out what you really have going for you. This is your natural, given, amazingly FREE stockpile of assets.

- Your marvelous eyes have a hundred million sensory receptors with which to enjoy the world. You can watch a sunset, read a book, or see a loved one. Count one asset!

- Through the courtesy of a complex, well-engineered hearing system you can listen beautifully. You can hear a concert, a waterfall, or a friendly voice. Count another asset!

– Your voice could (with ample training) speak any language in the world. You can laugh, whisper, or shout for joy. Count another asset!

– Your incredible body has over 500 muscles, 200 bones, and 60 miles of veins and arteries to serve you. Yet it tirelessly builds thousands of new cells daily and features a heart that beats over 100,000 times and pumps over 4,000 gallons a day without complaint. Count yet another asset!

– No computer, of any price, size, or style, has the complexity of your brain. Not even the most amazing super-computers with the most advanced robotics can perform tasks that a four-year-old can! Your brain controls millions of pain, touch, and temperature detectors all over your body, that can help you adjust to burning deserts, the sea, polar ice caps, outer space, and even classes at school!

You are the most complex creation the world has ever seen. You are the biological pinnacle of humankind. Never again complain that you need "something extra." You are one-of-a-kind and a unique biological event. Even identical twins have brains that think differently. Enjoy the rarity you have. Use your assets to become the student you know you can be.

STOP AND
TAKE ACTION

Develop confidence and faith in yourself through simple actions.

◆ Set up short, easily attainable goals for yourself and watch your successes pile up.

◆ Focus your memory and present thoughts on your virtues. This gives a stronger picture of yourself, thus building faith.

Another simple thing you can do every day is to read the Goal page in Chapter 13. The mind will accept anything as truth, if it is repeated and reinforced enough. It's great for building your confidence. Read it at night before bed, and in the morning, before starting your day. It's best read several times a day, as the messages can become a part of you even quicker. Scientists like sleep researcher Dr. Robert Stickgold of Harvard believe that down time for the brain is used to process thinking and learning and embed it into our permanent, long-term memory.

WHY GET SPECIALIZED SKILLS

There's no doubt that you have many special qualities. Just the fact that you are unique makes you special. One thing you can do to help reach your goals easier is to acquire special skills. In today's world, you'll need to be both a **generalist** (have an overall background about the local, national, and global trends) and a **specialist** (to be particularly good, as an expert, at something). These are the skills that will give you the extra confidence and make both school and your personal life easier.

As an example:

As a tenth grader at Hale High School, Scott was younger than many of his classmates, and lacked confidence. It's hard to have it in tenth grade where everyone seems older and bigger, and they act like they know their way around. But he had his goals set and knew what he wanted to achieve. His friend was a good wrestler and asked if he wanted to join the wrestling team. Scott had never wrestled before and was unsure if he could even make the team, much less compete. Fortunately, he made the junior varsity squad. He won only about half of his matches that year, but the confidence he gained by being part of a team was to last him for a lifetime.

Sign up for courses in memory and study skills, speed-reading, and test preparation. Learn from others who do it well. Develop a collection, a hobby, or computer skill. Join a dance class, learn to play an instrument, or go out for a school sports team. The worst that can happen is you'll end up where you are now—*not* on the team!

Then, discipline yourself to learn the habits you need to be a total success. Although you always can find someone who will tell you how hard school is or how tough certain classes are, ignore him or her. There are just as many others who juggle a full load of classes *and* still have time for fun. It can be done; you just need to commit yourself to doing it.

HOW TO USE "MIND-MOTIVATORS"

Motivation can be easy if you know how it works. You know you are already motivated to do certain things. After all, you got out of bed this morning, showered, dressed, ate, and now you are reading this book. "Big deal," you say, "anyone can do that." You're right. Except for one thing.

This means your mind *already* knows how to get you to do things. And the same things that get you motivated to do those ordinary things can also motivate you to do things like homework. It's simply a matter of finding out what your mind does to put you in motion, and that's pretty simple. But it'll take a bit of research on your part. Simply read this section all the way through, then go back and actually do the instructions. Close your eyes and think about an activity that you're very motivated to do. Pick something for which you constantly overcome obstacles to get yourself to do, such as working out, sports practice, a concert, a big date, preparing for something, or going on a vacation.

While you are thinking about yourself doing that activity, hold it in your mind. What kinds of feelings (if any) do you have about doing that activity? On a scale of 1 to 10 (1 is low), what's the intensity of them? Do you hear any sounds that get you motivated to do something? Is there a voice (do you tell yourself, "Now is the time!")? What are the qualities of that sound? Close up? Faraway? Which direction is that sound coming from? Low, high, fast, or slow? If you have a picture in your mind of doing that activity, are you seeing yourself "over there" in the picture, or are you seeing the activity out of your own eyes, while you are doing it? Is it a movie or a still frame? Is the activity close up or far away? In color or in black and white? Is it in 3-D or flat two-dimensional? Consider each of these qualities, then make up a list.

Your list is a record of how your mind motivates you to do something. As an example, you might find that when you are highly motivated to do something, you hear a loud booming voice coming from above your right ear. Then you see the positive outcome in 3-D, running like a color movie, and you are actually *in* the experience of doing it. Now, that's just an example. Your list of "motivational" mind qualities might be different, but it's worth its weight in gold to you.

The real secret to motivation is to find out how you work. For example, if, when you're motivated, you talk to yourself, what do you say or hear that gets you going? You might have a certain feeling, like a rushed-wind-at-your-back feeling. Can you bring that feeling back, for yourself, whenever you want to? Or you might get a mental picture, an image in your mind of the goal totally done. Or maybe the goal is undone and *that* gets you anxious and motivated. When you're ready to do school work, use the same words, feelings, or pictures that get you motivated for other things and you'll get fired up.

The skill levels of Mia Hamm, Tiger Woods, Lisa Leslie, or Kobe Bryant are certainly high. But the real reason they succeed so often is that they have learned to drive themselves by using their mental skills to achieve focus and motivate them toward their goals. You have to want it so badly you will settle for nothing less. By drawing upon your own knowledge of how you become motivated and applying the sensations and experiences of being highly inspired to your schoolwork, you will have gone from being a passenger on the "bus of life" to being the driver. That's pretty exciting!

HANDLING PERSONAL PROBLEMS

Did you ever notice that when it rains, it pours? Sometimes, it seems that everything that could happen, does. Major personal situations can certainly make life difficult. It's hard to concentrate, even with good study skills. Car problems, poor health, or romantic conflicts can be a hassle in life, but there is no reason why these should dominate. Outside events don't have to be catastrophes if you keep them in perspective. Most are really not the disasters they are made out to be.

One mistake consistently made in dealing with personal problems is avoiding them because of "over-thinking." This means making assumptions about what we perceive will or will not happen. These assumptions often immobilize an otherwise clear-thinking individual. If the problem involves someone else, it may be helpful to talk about your concern with the other person. Try to clear it up early. Be direct, honest, and warm. Communicate your feelings first, then your thoughts.

Listen to the other side before deciding upon a course of action. But take the situation into your hands and deal with it. Avoiding it only postpones it and amplifies the problem. Make an effort to not over-think or avoid personal problems, and they will become less worrisome for you. Most personal conflicts go away in time, but it's rarely worth it to wait that long.

Almost every school has a qualified counseling staff that can help you solve difficult problems. Then, why don't more people go? Counselors wonder, too! Usually, it's because people think they're the only ones having problems, so they're embarrassed. But that's a mistake. First, everyone has problems, from the very rich to the very poor, from the healthy to the sick, from the talented and smart, to the not so talented. If you're breathing, you have problems. The only time you don't have them is when you're dead! Get used to problems—they'll never go away. The only thing that changes is your ability to *deal* with problems. And the sooner you get skilled at it, the more fun and less stress you'll have in life. So, go see a school counselor if something's bugging you. Chances are good that the counselor has already dealt with and solved problems very similar to yours.

WHY DEVELOP PERSISTENCE

Nothing in the world can take the place of
  Persistence.
Talent will not; nothing is more common
  than unsuccessful men with talent.
Genius will not; unrewarded genius is almost
  a proverb.
Education will not; the world is full of educated
  failure.
Keep Believing.
Keep Trying.
Persistence and Determination alone are
  omnipotent.
                                        —Calvin Coolidge

Motivation is essential to begin the path to success, and persistence will keep you on that path. Motivation is like fuel for your car; it gets you going toward your goal. But cars will run out of gas unless the persistence is there to refuel. The starting point for developing persistence is to have something to persist *toward.* Have an exact and desirable goal in mind and keep it there. Your motivation will move you to action, and your persistence will keep you moving. Persistence is insured as long as you learn to cultivate it as a part of your character.

Successful people are so persistent they will simply not give up. They will explore and exhaust all possibilities and alternatives. Many problems go unsolved because someone gave up and lost the desire to continue. A genius does not wait for a magical bolt of inspiration. It takes hard work and long hours to produce results. Edison correctly said, "Genius is one percent inspiration and ninety-nine percent perspiration." And he should know. He holds more U.S. patents than any other man. Yet, he experienced thousands of failures in his career.

As an example:

The book you are now reading was originally turned down by 52 other publishers. Fortunately, the author had learned to persist. The fifty-third publisher, Barron's, published it, and it has since sold over 100,000 copies! You might be surprised how many authors (famous or not) have had a tough time getting their first work published. Be willing to invest your time and energy in something you believe in. Ideas don't work unless you do.

ACTION IS THE KEY

We've come a long way in this chapter. We've explored many ideas and strategies. Now, we're getting to the last of the principles of success—take action. It's pretty important, isn't it?

Every desire, every plan, every bit of knowledge is useless unless followed by action. No battle plan has ever won a war, no law ever prevented a crime, no book ever read itself. Action is the key. Repeat it to yourself over and over again. Action is the key. Do not wait for tomorrow. Do not wait for the time to be right. The time is right now. Do not worry about what to do, or how to do it. Just say when. Say now. Begin this moment—this precious moment, which will never come again. This priceless day, which will end in just a few hours, must be utilized. Live each day to the fullest through action.

STOP AND TAKE ACTION

◆ Make a list of the steps you could take in the next week that would help you get closer to your goal. Next, circle the ones that you could start up right away. Now, pick an idea, action, or strategy that you can start in on right away. That's your personal action that will begin your path to your dreams.

◆ Avoid procrastination. Get started early in the day,

while your energy level and motivation are high and your goals are clear. For today, just simply do it. Put your alibis and excuses away. Embrace life, laugh, and have fun. But most of all, act, and act now. Action is the only thing that will reap the rewards you want. It's the single most potent ingredient to success.

◆ Break down the task into small, manageable segments. Any task that seems daunting has a starting point, a middle, and an end. If you can't get it all done in a day, at least get started and make progress.

Review These Points

W-I-I-F-M? What's in It for Me?
Your Mind Naturally Seeks Goals
How to Make Goals Happen
How to Maintain Focus
Use Your Best Mind
How to Develop a Winning Attitude
Why Choose Friends Carefully
How to Build Faith in Yourself
Why Get Specialized Skills
How to Use "Mind-Motivators"
Handling Personal Problems
Why Develop Persistence
Action Is the Key

2
SUCCESS HABITS:
Smart Strategies

Do something once and it's just an action. Do something several times and you've got a pattern or routine. But do something day after day and you've got a habit. Habits are what make up our lifelong character. And it is our character, not lucky breaks or an easy-grading teacher, that makes our school success happen. The problem is, how do you get the right habits that form the right character to get the ball rolling?

As you know, habits can be formed randomly or purposely. Some students, just by circumstance, do something once by accident, then keep repeating it. If it's a good habit, all the better!

Now is a great time to start your successful habits. Once formed, they will be with you for years. In school, the successful habits you learn and use now will benefit you later for dozens of things outside of school. So, let's look at some of the important habits for school success.

LEARN HOW *YOU LEARN*

Everyone has a favorite way to learn. A learning style is a preferred way to learn. You may have noticed that, given a choice, you'd choose one way of learning over another: to listen, watch, or actually try something out. In other words, would you rather have someone tell you about a subject, read or watch a movie about it, or actually experience it happening, as in a science lab? These three styles are examples of auditory, visual, and kinesthetic learning.

- If you learn best by *listening*, you're what is called an **auditory learner.** You often don't *look* at the front of the room; you'll be more likely talking to yourself, inside your head. You use expressions like, "That *sounds* good." You often talk to others, tell stories or jokes, like to *hear* the ideas, not read about them. You may benefit by reviewing work with others and may even recall the sounds of what was said.

- If you know you are a **visual learner,** and your teacher talks a lot, you've got to find ways that you can *see* the information: video, books, magazines, chalkboard, handouts, notes, etc. You'll say phrases like, "I *see* what you mean." You like to write things down so you can *see* them. You like to sit where you can *see* the teacher, *see* what's on the board and you'll often *visualize* things inside your head. You're probably comfortable using graphic organizers or mind maps to *see* what you learn.

- If you're more active and have strong sensations about things, you're more likely a **kinesthetic learner.** In class, you go crazy having to stay so still; you'd rather get up and *do* something. You use expressions like: "That *feels* right." You might *play* sports, *do* art, drama, or other active hobbies. To learn, you might prefer to go to a lab class and do a hands-on activity. You might like the arts or physical education, too. You don't mind learning; you just like doing it in ways other than reading about it.

– There are other ways to categorize how you learn. You might be a **detail learner** or a more **global learner.** A teacher who talks, in order, following the lesson plan or format, who uses exact, specific examples may be much more interesting to you. If so, you're a **detail learner.**

– Teachers who skip around, tell stories, and try to relate the subject to big events, such as your life, their life, significant trends and issues, are more **global.** If you want to know why you are doing something before you do it, you are a **global learner.**

As an example:

Jason always seemed to have a tough time in classes, except the ones where he could *do* something. In the classes in which the teachers just stood and talked, or told everyone to read, he seemed to get bored and restless. But the ones in which he could get up and do things, like industrial arts, drama, science projects, or P.E. were always his favorite. He soon realized that he was not a slow or unmotivated learner; he was a kinesthetic learner. Once he figured this out, he started to use this information to his advantage. He would draw out what he learned from class on notes, posters, and doodles. He would act out things and work with other students on projects using role play and drama. This helped his learning come alive and he was less bored. As a result, he not only enjoyed school more, his grades also went up.

There are other learning styles, too, but these are enough for the moment. The point is simple. Start paying attention to how you learn best and begin to use that way to learn. You don't need to struggle or learn slowly. You have resources that you can use. Learning takes very little time. It's all the time wasted *not* learning that adds up to most students' study time. Learn your own "learning combination" by trial and error, test and retest. Go with your strengths; you've got plenty of them to succeed.

PREPARE YOURSELF

Your education can be measured in many ways, such as by increased knowledge, self-satisfaction, and monetary rewards. It's easy to add up the lifetime value of a high school or college education. Take the average working salaries of graduates and compare them with nongraduates. Then, multiply that amount over a lifetime. Compare the two. Let's say a high school graduate makes $40,000 a year and a college graduate earns $60,000 a year. That's a $20,000 difference, but over a lifetime of working from age 22 to 72, that's more than a *million* dollars more! If you are in college for four years at 220 days each year, that's 880 days of school. Divide 880 into a million and you get over $11,000 *per day* that going to school is worth to you. So it makes sense to start your school day by putting forth your best effort.

– Check over your personal appearance. We are all strongly influenced by our first impressions. That means grooming, personal hygiene, and clothes. Make the first impression a good one. Grooming means paying attention to your hair, nails, and general cleanliness and appearance. Wear clothes that fit, and that *don't* attract negative attention. No, you don't need to dress like a model or movie star but the right clothing can not only help your teacher feel that you're serious about school, it helps *you* feel more serious about it. By the way, just because your clothes say you want to learn, you can still have fun in how you dress!

– If the all-time best tool for learning is your brain, a close second must be computers. Given the direction of learning and technology, a computer is fast becoming a must. Today, some colleges require that you own a computer to even enter! If you don't have one now, there are two choices: Find out where you can rent one on an hourly basis (library, full-service copy shops, or media center) or keep your eyes and ears alert for a good used bargain.

– Make sure you have the tools you need to succeed. Have you got the books, papers, computer, or other supplies you'll need for class? It's frustrating to be all ready to go, and have no tools. Make sure you keep a year-long calendar with you for scheduling. Then, you can not only avoid over-scheduling but also make sure you have allowed time for the more important events in your life (pizza and a movie?).

BOOST YOUR SELF-IMAGE

How do you see yourself? Do you think of yourself as a good or poor student? Your actions, feelings, and behavior are pretty consistent with your conception of yourself. What's great is, it can be changed. There are thousands of students who see themselves as poor students, feel that way, hang around other poor students, and consequently get poor grades. Why? They prove themselves right by becoming the "failures" they thought they were.

Don't confuse self-image with positive thinking. They are not the same. Positive thinking is believing that things will turn out well whether it's plausible or not. But by improving your self-image, you are getting at the source, the only thing you have true control over— yourself. What you say to yourself when you talk to yourself, how you think of yourself, and how you feel about yourself all create your personality and character.

Whatever kind of person you would like to be, or whatever changes you would like to make, the change has to come from within. Focus on being the person you want to be. Get strong mental pictures about the student you want to be. *See* yourself doing what is necessary for total success. *Hear* yourself saying the things that top students say. *Feel* yourself being confident and taking action that leads to your next success. This process helps you create the character you want to become. It also helps you make the transition to stronger character. By becoming comfortable with the future you, your subconscious can begin to direct your thoughts and actions accordingly. The purpose of a creative mental picture is simple. First, it enables you to see the end product, and thereby become comfortable with the new you. Your new mental picture can actually provide you with a "mental mold" or model for your actions by keeping the desired behavior in mind. You will become what you think about, dream about, and desire to be the most.

To take advantage of your mind's ability to help you succeed, practice what you wish to become, not what you are now. That's the second benefit of mental pictures. You can become the person for whom you act out the role. Most of us have already done this role-playing in one form or another. Often, movie actors find that by playing one role for too long, they actually do take on characteristics of that role. Playing a role can actually help you become it!

WHAT TO DO NOW

Three things are critical:

1. Stop comparing yourself with others. Don't listen to anyone else comparing you with them. You are unique in all the world. Any comparison with others is ridiculous. The only comparison you should be making is how you are doing compared with yourself, a month ago, a year ago, etc. Now *that's* a useful comparison. If you're improving, you're being a success.

2. The next thing that builds self-esteem is integrity. That means, among other things, living up to your values. If you value honesty, be honest. If you value friends, treat your friends well. If you value success, then get on the path. The secret is to set short goals and meet them, set another short goal and meet that one, too.

3. The third thing to help build self-esteem is to believe in yourself. Proper mental picturing takes about two minutes a day. Sit or lie comfortably, and close your eyes. Use your imagination to create a strong, clear picture of yourself doing the desired activity. Make the picture come alive, imagining the sights and sounds of yourself successfully studying. Picture yourself zipping through a textbook, giving a great report in class, or getting an A on a test. Sound strange? Remember this: If you can't even imagine yourself getting A's, what hope is there for the real thing?

To become an A student, you've first got to believe it's possible. Associate with other good students and acquire the study skills taught in this book. Big-time success can be yours as soon as you see yourself as an A student because you *are* one when you believe in yourself.

Visualize A's, Not Z's

READ, READ, AND READ

With television everywhere, it seems it's the exception when someone's reading. Everybody tells you to read—even ads on television! Read, read, read, they say. But why get the reading habit? Reading stimulates the mind. It helps you learn a wider variety of things than you could ever hear about or experience. It also lets you use your imagination. Reading can help make you more creative in solving life's problems, for instance. In fact, the inventor Thomas Edison was such a hungry reader that he had literally read thousands of books. This gave him the background to be able to become one of the world's greatest inventors.

As an example:

> Kerry was not a good reader. She kept hearing about a speed-reading and study skills course. She was skeptical, but she was also desperate. She never finished her assigned reading, and studying took too much time. Her parents said they'd pay for the course, so she gave it a try. Kerry would have to say that she honestly didn't give it the effort she should have. She never learned to read by zipping down the pages as they showed in the commercial. But she did learn better ways to organize her thinking and notes, and to read much faster. Within six months, her grades were up a bit and school did get easier.

If you commonly don't understand or forget what you read, seek help. If reading has always been a struggle, it's not too late to get assistance. Your school may have a counselor or testing service to help you to understand the best form of intervention for you. At times, an evaluation may reveal that someone has a reading-based learning disability. This is important information, since there are many strategies that can be implemented to help a person compensate for such a difficulty.

If you get help, and learn to read better, you may relieve your anxiety about reading. And once you learn to read well, you'll read more. That's important, because most of what you need to know is in print form. Once you're satisfied with your reading skills, use them. Read as much as you can, and read material with varying levels of difficulty. It's not enough to read the morning newspaper if you want to be really well read. Read text-books, nonfiction best-sellers, and magazines. The important thing is to read as much as you can.

EAT SMARTER

Your diet strongly affects your moods, energy levels, and thinking ability. In her book, *Your Miracle Brain*, Jean Carper said that what you eat and when you eat it can make a big difference in your learning. By taking better care of the inside of yourself, you can increase your chances for success on your report card. How? Better foods lead to greater concentration and problem-solving skills. You'll be able to focus longer and read better. Foods can even help you feel more positive.

- Ideally, you'll stay with a low-sugar, low-salt, and low-fat diet.
- Eat several small meals a day instead of fewer large meals.

- Drink about six to eight glasses of pure water each day (soft drinks don't count).

- Drink fewer liquids with your meals and, instead, eat food higher in water content such as salads, vegetables, and pasta.

- Eat at least one half of your vegetables fresh and uncooked.

- Keep whole grains and natural foods in your diet.

- Cook foods with more herbs, lemon juice, and spices, and less salt.

- Eat slowly.

- Need an energy boost? Get your sugars from fructose, the sugar in fruits. Eat a banana, apple, peach, pear, tangerine, orange, or kiwi fruit.

Need to relax? A high carbohydrate meal with calcium (milk or other dairy product) will calm you by raising your levels of tryptophan and serotonin, both calm-inducers. Peanuts do the same. If you need to do a lot of studying and thinking, there's a science to it. Neurotransmitters—the brain's chemical messengers— are created from the protein in your food. Make sure that you have enough protein (and the right kinds) for healthy thinking. Before studying, eat a light protein-rich meal, possibly with yogurt, nuts, eggs, turkey, or fish. To remember what you study, eat foods that help the release of tyrosine, choline, and phenylalanine—the neurotransmitters associated with thinking and memory. These include milk, nuts, bananas, seeds, rice, and oats.

Does when you eat foods matter? Yes, it does. If you're going to eat carbos or sugars, eat proteins first.

That means, eat eggs or yogurt with your breakfast. In general, eat your proteins earlier in the day and your carbos and sugars later in the day. A pizza with meat and cheese (protein) is better for thinking than just a crust by itself. The proteins are perfect for school; the carbos are perfect for your active life after 3:00 P.M. By eating smarter, you'll also *feel* smarter, and get better grades. Now, what's one change you can make to eat smarter?

List it here: _____

ATTEND CLASSES REGULARLY

Should you ever miss class? Most of the time, no. But actually, there are times when missing class makes sense. For example, when ill health makes it inadvisable to attend. Regular attendance assures you'll have all the necessary lecture notes for exams, and allows you the opportunity to clear your understanding of any text-book reading while it's still fresh in your mind. Get to class on time. It irritates teachers when late students interrupt the class. If you quickly grasp a concept and find yourself distracted as the teacher clarifies the information for other students, you might want to refocus yourself by simply reviewing your notes from the previous day or formulating new questions. Then you can still make good use of your time.

Arriving early will allow you to get the seat you want near the front of the class. Sitting in the front will help you hear more easily, see visual aids clearly, and show your teacher you're interested in the class. Pay attention and lean forward in class. It's better to take too many notes than not enough. Why? Notetaking keeps your mind engaged on the subject. Otherwise, you wander off and, pretty soon, you'll wonder if you ought to bother to write something down. As you take notes, you should develop a code for highlighting the key points. This may take the form of underlining phrases, putting stars in certain margins, putting words in bold or in all capitals, and so on. If you experiment, you will see what system works most effectively for you. And then be sure to *review* your notes!

KNOW YOUR TEACHER

Learning is about relationships. It's relationships between ideas, between concepts, and between numbers. It's about relationships between formulas, theories, strategies, and tools. It's also about relationships between you and your material, you and the school, you and your friends, and, finally, you and the teacher. The old way of education was more adversarial: It was you "against" the teacher. The teacher would try to be aloof and distant, and the students would try to "out-smart" the teacher to figure out what's on the test. While that old model still exists, there's less and less of that attitude today. Get to know your teacher after class and develop positive communication.

Clear up difficult points from class lectures and give your teacher feedback on lecture material and presentation. Most instructors really appreciate knowing how well their material is coming across. It's often beneficial to discover your teacher's style of teaching and topic preferences. What is his or her favorite way of teaching, favorite subject, or author?

In short, it's OK to specialize your approach by appealing to what your teacher or professor asks for. Some students may think, "What an apple polisher!" But wait a minute. You have two objectives in school: to get a degree and to learn as much as you can while doing it. No one wants to be this blunt about it, but it's true—those who succeed are good at playing the system. If a better teacher relationship gets you to learn more, and it works in the system, you're doing some good for everyone.

MAKE A SCHEDULE

Some straight A students have exact, written-out schedules. Should you use one? Generally, yes. There's too much going on for you to realistically think you'll recall every class, assignment, name, date, or event with just a prayer. Here are some of the more obvious clues: If you lose track of key dates or appointments, use a schedule. If you don't have a near-photographic memory, use a schedule. If your life is complicated or changes a lot, use a schedule. If you have a tendency to procrastinate, use a schedule.

Those who need schedules will find that they can pinpoint effective times for study. A schedule can help remind you of your school commitments and prevent careless oversights. A weekly study schedule should include a general list of your major time commitments. Include classes, athletics, work schedules, or social engagements. Keep this weekly schedule to make sure the obvious is not forgotten. Then keep a daily appointment, errand, and To Do list of smaller commitments.

Many students like the hand-held devices for scheduling. Others find that a calendar works fine. Whichever tool you use for scheduling, you should look at it at the end of the day, cross off or delete those things you've completed, and carry the remaining tasks over to the next day. This increases goal orientation and builds your success image through daily achievement. Your assignment, if you haven't already done so, is to get a calendar and begin planning out this coming month. When will you do it?

Write the answer here: _____

DEVELOP CONCENTRATION

Some students seem to have amazing concentration. Concentration helps you to use your time better and accomplish more. How can you do it? Here are some surefire concentration strategies:

– Find the right time to study. Some students are night people—those who are just getting ready to study around midnight—whereas others prefer daylight.

– Find the proper place for studying by using the same desk all the time, if possible. The same desk creates familiarity and comfort, which aids in getting started. Use either natural lighting (daytime) or incandescent lighting (a regular lightbulb, not fluorescent).

– Set goals—short-term goals, goals for pages done, for chapters done, for project completion—just set goals! Set realistic goals. Don't tell yourself, "I'm not getting out of this chair until I know this entire chemistry book." Rather, set a realistic goal such as, "I'm going to learn chapters six and seven within an hour." Focus energy on just one topic at a time. If you have a project to complete, for instance, about a famous person from the Civil War, and you have a week to finish it, try not to wait until the last night to begin. Break down the task into manageable portions. On days one and two, you might want to research the person by reading your class textbook, looking for information on the computer, and reading through books at the library. On day three, you may want to gain more information about the time in history in which the person lived. Then, on day four, you can begin outlining your paper. On day five, develop a rough draft. This leaves you with days six and seven to create the finished paper. Segmenting an assignment in a fashion similar to this may make the project less overwhelming and easier to accomplish. Try to see if this strategy works for you.

– Drink water. It prevents dehydration and keeps your attention and memory sharp (see page 65).

– Make sure you keep your studying active. Read, take notes, read, think, take notes. Never go more than a page or two without making what you learn into an active process.

– Take short breaks every 15 to 30 minutes. Get up and stretch, stick your head outside and get some fresh air. Harvard medical doctor Allan Hobson suggests taking a short power nap of 5 to 15 minutes during your natural energy lull, between 1 and

3 P.M. This serves to resupply the level of amines to the brain. Those are the chemical source of our attention and arousal.

- Remove the usual distractions, such as a phone, calendar of upcoming events, television, and pinups. Anything you have that stimulates daydreaming will destroy your concentration.

- The ideal noise for study is white noise, a term used to describe a low-level background sound that masks outside distractions. Ideally, you can use instrumental music, a bubbling aquarium, or even a steady traffic flow. These noises help equalize the extremes of dead quiet and unbearable annoyances. It takes special concentration to eliminate the mental clutter that often impairs good study habits. Any obvious impediment to concentration should be removed.

- Before concentration is automatic, take care of any immediate needs such as hunger, outside noises, poor lighting, etc. Once you learn to concentrate, you'll be pleased to find that it becomes a habit. And that makes it easier the next time.

REDUCE STUDY STRESS

Anticipate deadlines and complete papers and projects well in advance. This serves the dual purpose of ensuring assignment completion and allowing for the possibility of its review or revision. If your paper is due on the sixteenth, finish it by the tenth or twelfth. Then, if your schedule suddenly gets crowded or hectic, there's no anxiety about getting it in on time. And if you get any new ideas, you'll still have time to include them in your assignment.

Take advantage of recent brain research. In the book *The Chemistry of Conscious States*, Hobson suggested studying right before short naps and right before sleeping. This allows your mind to better use the sleep state to strengthen your memory of the material. In the relaxed sleep or dream state, your mind can resort, recreate, and review material so that it becomes even more powerful and clear the next morning. Study or review immediately before sleeping. Then tell yourself that you wish to think about it. In time, you'll be using your sleep states for greater success.

USE A CONSISTENT STUDY AREA

It helps to study in familiar places all the time because it enables you to develop a quick consistent pattern for concentration. Otherwise, you may spend the first twenty minutes of your study time getting familiar with a new desk, chair, room, scenery, and passersby. Generally, it's not advisable to study on your bed because it's so comfortable that you may end up sleeping instead of studying. Study in an area where the lighting is indirect, yet strong; it should also be reasonably quiet. Make sure the book you are reading is 14 to 18 inches from your eyes. By keeping your book at this distance, eye fatigue will be lessened.

PSYCH OUT OPPONENTS

Who are your opponents? They are the demons of studying, such as distractions, hunger, restlessness, and confusion. A sloppy mental attitude can kill good intentions. Everyone's got some kind of schoolwork or task they don't want to do. Instead of complaining, tell yourself, "I'm going to get this material and get it fast." Decide on what you need to learn and how much time it will take you to cover the required material. If you approach your task with a positive, receptive, open mind, the work will go much faster. If you *believe* you can move through the text rapidly, half the battle is won.

There is an almost unlimited number of distractions that mysteriously pop up just before studying. At times, studying seems so boring that almost anything is more interesting. Learn to avoid such prestudy tactics as preparing a snack, staring at the ceiling, watching TV, surfing the Internet, visiting friends, or talking on the phone. Most things are done out of habit, not out of need, so think about whether you really need those usual rituals. Form consistent positive study habits of getting assigned work done on time. Only then will you become the master of your school habits.

STUDY BITE-SIZED CHUNKS

One of the great stoppers to getting started is the amount of studying to do. After all, who wants to sit down to study for two or three hours on a beautiful day? The answer is simple, if you keep this statement about the brain in mind: It is easier to "act your way into feeling" than to "feel your way into acting."

As an example:

At one school, an athlete realized this problem and came up with a solution. On cold winter mornings, he rarely felt like getting up to work out. So he said, "I'll get dressed, then see how I feel." He put on his sweatshirt and sweatpants. Then he felt okay, so he put on his running shoes. After that, he still felt okay, so he put on his gloves and wool hat. Then he said, "I'll just take a short walk." So he started out. After a while, the cold invigorating morning air awakened him even more. So he began to run. The more he ran, the more loose and energetic he felt. In a short time, he was up to full speed and promptly completed his workout. The funny part is, he *never* really felt like doing it—he only felt okay *at each interim step* along the way!

That means that it is better to start doing a small chunk of homework than to wait for a bolt of inspiration out of the blue. That "bolt" rarely happens. If you've got two chapters to do, just promise yourself that you'll do an overview. Then, at the end of the overview, if you're getting into it, do more. Above all, don't let yourself get discouraged by thick books or imposing titles.

Set up short, easily attainable goals and count your successes as you move unhesitatingly through even the toughest material. Almost any material can be broken up into a format style. Separate difficult reading into categories—for example, introduction, examples, background, opinions, and facts. Then the material will become much more readable. One step at a time. Inch by inch, it's a cinch. Nothing big and grand needed. Just bite off a small, chewable chunk and do it. No excuses, no procrastination. Begin your work now and it'll get done.

PUT BALANCE IN YOUR LIFE

At this time of your life, you've got a lot to juggle: academics, fitness, relationships, chores, school activities, finances, hobbies, sports, and health. One thing you can be sure of is that: life requires that you pay attention to every part of it. If you ignore your health, you can almost expect illness. If you ignore your relationships, you can expect upsets. And it's the same for each of the other areas. The moral is simple: Organize your activities. Make sure you set aside time to play, time to work out, time for planning, time for homework, and time for friends and family. Take care of promises and commitments. Life offers much, but it demands much, too. Plan your work and work your plan. Anything less will come back to you in the form of trouble. But if you stand up to the challenge, you'll experience lower stress and have more fun every day.

Review These Points

Learn *How* You Learn
Prepare Yourself
Boost Your Self-image
Read, Read, and Read
Eat Smarter
Attend Classes Regularly
Know Your Teacher
Make a Schedule
Develop Concentration
Reduce Study Stress
Use a Consistent Study Area
Psych Out Opponents
Study Bite-sized Chunks
Put Balance in Your Life

3
YOUR LEARNING ENVIRONMENT

We never work, think, or play in a vacuum; it's always in some kind of context. That means there's a location and there are some kind of circumstances. These have a direct biological, sociological, and psychological impact on you, and therefore on the results of your reading. Where you learn may be just as important as how you learn. As you set up your reading environment, whether at home or in an office, give yourself every chance you can to succeed.

SETTING UP THE BEST LEARNING ENVIRONMENT

Proper Lighting

How much does the lighting matter? Research suggests that it matters a great deal. Dr. Wayne London's 1988 experiments caught worldwide attention. London, a Vermont psychiatrist, switched the lighting in three elementary school classrooms halfway through the school year. He was curious about whether the type of lighting mattered to the students. During the December holiday break, he changed the current fluorescent lighting to Vitalite full-spectrum lighting. Although the experiment was not a double blind one, no one expected any particular result.

The results, however, were amazing. London found that the students who were in the classrooms with full-spectrum lighting missed fewer school days than those in the other classrooms. London said, "Ordinary fluorescent light has been shown to raise the cortisol level in the blood, a change likely to suppress the immune system." This affects other areas in learning.

Some 160,000 school-age children were studied to determine which, if any, environmental factors influenced their learning. The results of his research were amazing. By the time they graduated from elementary school (ages 11 to 12), over 50 percent of the student subjects had developed deficiencies related to classroom lighting!

To test the hypothesis, changes were made in the students' learning environment, and the same children were studied six months later. The results of the change were equally dramatic: Visual problems were reduced 65 percent, fatigue was reduced 55 percent, infections decreased 43 percent, and posture problems dropped 25 percent. In addition, those same students showed a dramatic increase in academic achievement.

Current research suggests that the best lighting for reading is low to moderate levels of natural lighting. The second best choice is full-spectrum fluorescent or incandescent lighting. Indirect lighting is best, since it keeps eye fatigue lowest. Do what you can to provide the best lighting for yourself. You may be surprised how something so simple can return such big rewards.

Cool Temperatures

How much does temperature affect your reading? Dr. Robert Ornstein, author of *The Healing Brain*, reported in a book titled *The Psychology of Consciousness*, that the brain is far more efficient with a three-degree temperature decrease than a three-degree temperature increase from a baseline of 72°F. In U.S. Defense Department studies, Taylor and Orlansky reported that heat stress dramatically lowers scores in both intellectual and physical tasks. High temperatures were responsible for decreases in performance requiring accuracy, speed, dexterity, and physical acuity. While many types of obstacles and barriers are known to reduce or impair learning, heat stress is one of the most preventable. Keep your reading environment cool (not cold) for best attention, focus, and comprehension. For most learners, this means in the 65 to 70°F range.

Pleasant Surroundings

Our brains make connections and associations with almost everything, some of them good, others not so good. We connect feelings to people, places, objects, and events. A photograph, a chair, a face, a song, an activity, or even a plant can bring back a specific memory or release a whole flood of positive or negative memories. It makes sense to do everything in your power to have more positive than negative associations with what you see in your reading environment.

Scientists at the National Aeronautics and Space Administration have discovered that the use of plants creates a better scientific, learning, and thinking environment for astronauts. Could their same research apply to learners indoors? The former head of the Environmental Research Laboratory said that certain plants have improved life for the astronauts, as well as for his own personal life at home. He said that they remove pollutants from the air, increase the negative ionization, and charge it with oxygen. In fact, according to the Federal Clean Air Council, studies have shown that plants raised the oxygen levels and increased productivity by 10 percent. The top five plants for removing toxins and cleaning the air are dracenas, spiders, ficus, palms, and rubber plants.

In addition, minimize distractions (both visual and auditory) when you read so that you will not be disturbed. You might unplug a phone or put on an answering machine. You might do your reading in a place that allows you to concentrate, or put a "Do Not Disturb" sign on the door. Does your specific study location matter? Only to the degree that you either do well in it or you don't. Find a good location and stick to it.

Specific Aromas

While you can tune out certain sounds like traffic or an air conditioner, smells are different. They are processed directly by the mid-brain area (hypothalamus). This means we get the full impact of aromas before we've had a chance to even think about them. In *Advanced Aromatherapy*, Dr. Kurt Schnaubelt suggested using pure (not artificial) aromas and avoiding most of the commercial aromas. According to Dr. Schnaubelt, commercial aromas may be diluted or contaminated and won't give you the effect you want. Some of the safer ones, as well as those scents that are influential in mental alertness and in relaxation are:

Mental alertness	Relaxation
lemon	lavender
cinnamon	orange
peppermint	rose

It turns out that several specific scents can positively stimulate our attention and memory. Two of the best are lemon and peppermint. How do you get these into your environment? You can buy lemon or peppermint oils and put them on, in, or near a fan, heater, or candle. You can also use room fresheners that have these aromas. Although the processed effects are not for everyone, you might be pleasantly surprised by how well they work for you. In general, the pure ones are best.

Appropriate Music

Can listening to music help you learn? It may depend on who's doing the listening. For about 20 percent of students, music seems to be an annoyance and they do better with a quiet study area. For these students, the music stays in their head and becomes highly distracting. For the remaining 80 percent, the answer seems to be yes, it can be helpful.

If you are going to listen to music, there are two ways to go. One is to use music that you like (such as a local radio station or your favorite CDs). The value in this is simple: Music you like keeps you awake, keeps your spirits up, and helps the time go by faster. If you're sharp enough to *not* sound out the words in your head (you just like the rhythm and beat), this might be a good way to go.

The second method is to use music as background sound. However, because most music is composed to be listened to, the trick is to find music that does not "hook in" your mind and invite you to pay close attention to it. In other words, the best background music is highly predictable. It's music that you know is there and it does some good, but it doesn't occupy your thoughts. Which music is this? Typically it's nature sounds (such as waterfalls, ocean waves, or the rain forest) or smooth jazz (such as George Benson, David Sanborn, Rick Braun). You might also like some types of music from the Baroque era (1600–1720). This predictable, productive music was composed by artists such as Bach, Handel, Corelli, Haydn, and Vivaldi. Get CDs with an orchestra, not one or two instruments. You might create your own custom CD using only music in a major key and at a faster pace (andante, not adagio or largo).

How does music help us learn? It activates both sides of the brain. It elicits emotional responses, regulates attentional states, and stimulates the limbic system. The limbic system and the subcortical region of the brain are involved in engaging musical and emotional responses. More important, research has documented the role of the brain's hippocampus in long-term memory. This means that when information is imbued with music, there's a greater likelihood that the brain will encode it into long-term memory.

Proper Reading Posture

How you sit affects how you feel, which, in turn, affects your attitude about what you read as well as how you read it. Generally, the best posture for reading is sitting upright with your back straight or bent slightly forward. Lying down, lounging, or slouching may impair alertness and concentration. Sit at a table, resting the book at about a 45-degree angle from the table. This gives your eyes a clear, full view of the whole page and considerably decreases eyestrain. You might place a two-to-three inch-thick book or notebook under the book you are reading. Most of the time, books are a bit too close to the eyes. If you have good vision, corrected or not, you might find less eyestrain by placing a book a few inches further away.

Negatively Charged Air

All air, inside or outside, has an electrical charge. These charged particles are called ions. When it comes to air, the more negatively charged it is, the better. Smoke, dust, smog, pollutants, electrical emissions, heating systems, coolers, and traffic can all be harmful. With these, the air becomes more highly electrified (too many positive ions) and humans react. Studies suggest that between 57 and 85 percent of the population is strongly affected by these ions and can gain dramatically from more negative ions.

The impact of negatively charged air on the body is powerful. Originally, it was found to speed recovery in burn or asthma patients. It was later discovered to affect serotonin levels in the bloodstream, to stabilize alpha rhythms, and to positively impact our reactions to sensory stimuli. Ornstein reported that rats exposed to negative ionization grew a 9 percent larger cerebral cortex. In other words, the electrical charge in the air boosted brain size! The greater levels of alertness can translate to improved learning. There are nearly 800 research papers on the effects of negatively ionized air. (A researcher at RCA Laboratories first stumbled on the ion effect in 1932.)

Dr. Kornblueh, of the American Institute of Medical Climatology, was among the first to demonstrate the dramatic effect that the electrical charge in the air has on our behavior. His work at the University of Pennsylvania's Graduate Hospital and at Northeastern and Frankford hospitals in Philadelphia led him to make such charges a permanent part of hospital treatments. Many corporations, including ABC, Westinghouse, General Electric, Carrier, Philco, and Emerson now use ion generators in the workplace.

What can you do to increase the negative ionization of the air you breathe? Several things can help:

- Increase the number of live plants around you.

- Get fresh outside air in your environment.

- Sit near indoor aquariums, waterfalls, or humidifiers.

Mobility

Many learners feel compelled to stay seated to learn. It's almost as if the ghost of a teacher is lurching over them. But, some research indicates you may actually learn better by moving around often. You might want to get up and walk around while you think things through. You might want to sit in a way that you can tap your feet or rock your chair. Mobility, even simply standing up, can boost learning.

Dr. Max Vercruyssen of the University of Southern California discovered how your body's posture affects learning. His research showed that, on the average, standing increased heartbeats by ten extra times per minute. That sends more blood to the brain, which activates the central nervous system to increase neural firing. Researchers found that, on the average, there's a 5 to 15 percent greater flow of blood and oxygen to the brain when standing. Could you place a book on a countertop, and, while standing, read for a couple of minutes? You may be surprised at how well it works. Before you decide one way or another, give it a try.

Hydration

Surprisingly, the average learner is often dehydrated. This dehydration leads to poor learning performance. Your brain works on a complex electrolyte formula that requires the ideal balance, just like a car battery. Too much or too little sodium or potassium can be disastrous to your brain. Fortunately, those are well regulated by your own automatic mechanisms. Water, however, is another story.

Some learning specialists recommend from eight to twelve glasses a day, depending on your body size, the weather, and your activity level. But six to eight may be more practical. Nutritionists recommend pure water to ensure that it is free of contaminants. It's also better to have pure water, rather than coffee or tea because these act as diuretics that cause your body to need even more water to make up the deficit. Teachers have found that in classrooms where students are encouraged to drink water as often as needed, behavior improves, as does performance. Cut down on the amount of soft drinks, tea, or coffee you consume. Start replacing these liquids with a simple glass of water. You'll be pleased with the difference.

MIND BREAKS

The mind is very poor at maintaining a continuous, sustained focus; it's better at short bursts. Sometimes your reading bursts might be ten minutes, other times as long as 30 to 50 minutes, but it's rarely longer than that. Feel free to take short breaks. They are normal and natural ways for the brain to balance the varied effects of nutrition, hormones, and environmental stimuli.

Breaks ensure that your concentration will stay high. They also help you take advantage of the brain's memory cycles. Many students have found an egg timer, a stopwatch, or digital watch useful in keeping to a close schedule. Others let their body's own natural rhythms tell them when it's time to stop. Experiment and you'll find out which is best for you.

What do you think? Are your learning conditions optimal? While the conditions are not the only thing that make the difference between a poor and excellent learner, they are something that you have some control over.

STOP AND TAKE ACTION

◆ You can do it right now. Take a few minutes. Before you go any further, do what you can to set up your ideal environment.

◆ What I can and will do right away:_____

_____

◆ What I can and will do within 30 days:_____

_____

Review These Points

Setting Up the Best Learning Environment
Proper Lighting
Cool Temperatures
Pleasant Surroundings
Specific Aromas
Appropriate Music
Proper Reading Posture
Negatively Charged Air
Mobility
Hydration

Mind Breaks

STUDY STRATEGIES:
How to Get It Done, and Get It Right

If you're anywhere close to an average student, you'll spend thousands of hours studying from first through twelfth grade. This *huge* amount of time can be reduced considerably through smart study skills. But many students have never really been taught *how* to study. Studying is a process some schools may expect you to learn on your own. And because it is not always taught, *this is the most important chapter in the book for you.* This process will help you *every time* you study from now on. Learn it and use it!

Smart studying does not simply consist of reading, underlining, and rereading. Your new study process consists of a brain-smart set of strategies designed to make the learning come alive. It is based on the multilayered learning process, and may actually take less time than your old method of studying. It may seem longer at first, but each step takes less time, and because it is so well structured, you will have better success at test time. Here we go: The following is your surefire study plan.

STUDY BY P-A-G-E—PREPARE, ASK, GATHER, AND EVALUATE

Time and again, students have proved that a multilayered study plan is much more effective than spend-

The System:

Prepare

Ask

Gather

Evaluate

It's Easy with P–A–G–E!

ing all their time reading and highlighting. The only way to learn the material is to become actively involved in absorbing and integrating it. Studying is an active process, not a passive one. So get pumped up—you're ready to learn!

Prepare Your Mind

How do you prepare your mind? Many ways will work. Start with these simple suggestions:

- Get rid of distractions. Do your best to reduce the amount of paper on your desk, distracting pictures, calendars, or other clutter.
- Keep the music low or off.
- Make sure the phone won't disturb you.
- Put a *Quiet* sign on your door.
- Find a place to read or study that puts you in a good, upright, active learning posture.
- Have some drinking water on your desk.
- Wear loose clothes.
- Get rid of any distracting thoughts by writing them down and assigning a next step to them so you can focus on your work. For example, if you are upset with someone, write down how you were wronged, what you want to say to them, and how they could make it right. Sometimes, all you want is an apology or just to be listened to.
- Make sure your room is at the right temperature, with cool (not cold) air, good circulation, and good lighting.

– Pull out your study materials and organize them. Figure out what you have, what you're missing.

– Take out your assignment.

– Take in a big deep breath and relax.

Finally, you're ready to go. Now, get out your materials, and start browsing.

Why browse? It primes your mind for future learning. The brain is poorly designed for brand-new big ideas or concepts. But it is very good at nibbling at ideas that become big ideas. Browsing provides the mind with the hooks through preexposure to a topic. It is almost as if it gives your brain little Velcro stickers or mental Post-its with which to snag information later on.

What to browse. Browse through the resources you need for your classes. These resources include, but are not limited to, the following:

– CD-ROM files

– Textbooks

– The Internet

– Library books

– Video stores for documentary videos

– Museums, fairs, science projects

– Your home

– Magazines, journals, newsletters

– Class notes

How you browse. The process is simple:

- Locate your sources.
- Take no more than five to thirty seconds per page to glance over the material.
- Note all headlines, subtitles, and graphics. See if they have what you want.
- Make a mental note about what is located where, so you can go back later to dig into the source.

For example, in a textbook you'll want to get an overview. Start by turning pages quickly to scan the information. Gather short answers to the following questions:

1. What are the main topics?
2. What do I already know about these topics?
3. What special terminology is used to present the topics?
4. Who is the author?
5. How is the book organized?
6. How difficult is the material?

Create a mental map. Have you ever tried (or would you even dare) to put together a jigsaw puzzle without knowing the picture on the outside of the puzzle box? It would be nearly hopeless! Your brain learns very poorly with isolated fragments of information. But it learns very well when you know the big picture. How do you get the equivalent of the picture on the puzzle box? It's simple. You take a few moments and draw the pieces. Do you need to be an artist? No. If you've got paper, pencil, and any ideas at all, you can create a mental map of the material.

Begin to structure your thinking around the design of the book. Decide how much material you wish to learn. Draw a picture of the organization of it. You can use fish-bone diagrams, recall patterns, neuro-maps, or simply put the more important information to the left, details to the right. Leave more room under topics and titles that have more pages involved. Draw these maps and lines before reading, to help your mind better organize and store the data. After a chapter or section, go back and add to your notes. Here is a sample of this:

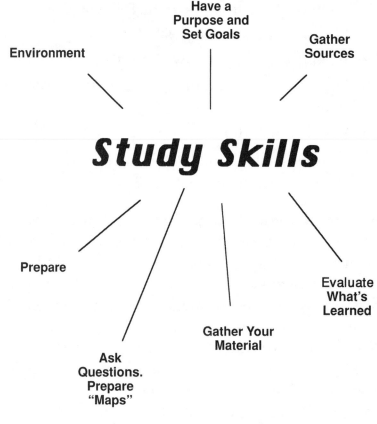

FIGURE 4-1

On a computer, you might do some scrolling down the document. Find the table of contents or you can even do searches for key words. You might stop at the more interesting parts and give them a closer look. Make a mental note of what's available and where it's located. Once you've finished this initial step, the browsing part is done.

Ask Questions

The browsing process does many important things for your learning, especially planting the seed for learning. But now it's time to start to get your brain in full gear. Since the mind works very well at finding answers to questions, let's start first with asking questions. The more questions you ask, the more ways you've primed your mind to find answers. You've already browsed through the material, so you know what's easy and what's hard. You already know where the meat of the material is and where the fluff is. Now, let's start with the real learning.

We'll now go on a hunt for questions in your material. Move quickly, skimming through the chapter much faster than at your usual reading rate. Your purpose here is to find out what is important and how it is presented, *not to read it.*

You'll have two categories of questions. The **first group** that comes up helps you stand back and identify what you need and want from the material. Here are examples of questions that can and should form part of your prereading habit:

- What is my final application of this reading material?

- How important is this material to me. In other words, what specifically is that value?

- What are the teacher's expectations?

- Do I want to recall very specific facts and other details?

The **second group** of questions you'll ask is more content-related. In order to be able to ask powerful prereading questions, you'll want to first scan the material very quickly. Check all boldfaced headings, *turning each into a question* you will answer later. Here are some examples:

- **Heading/Chapter Subtitle:**
  Computer Modeling

- **Your possible questions:**
  What is computer modeling?
  How does it work?
  Why should I know about it?

- **Heading/Chapter Subtitle:**
  Genes and Disease

- **Your possible questions:**
  Whose genes and which diseases?
  What's new in this field?
  Why should I care about this now?

- **Heading/Chapter Subtitle:**
  Technology and Modern Wars

- **Your possible questions:**
  What technology? Which wars?
  What role does technology play in wars?
  What do I really need to know about this?

- **Heading/Chapter Subtitle:**
  Lines, Vectors, and Triangles

- **Your possible questions:**
  What's the official definition of a line?
  How will I use these concepts?

Use trigger words. Have you ever noticed while you were reading that certain words seemed to **jump** off the page and ask for attention? There's a good chance that those words are keys to the author's message. "Hey, look at me," they seem to say. Those trigger words are key words—easy-to-spot, repeatedly used terms that present themes, vocabulary, and central ideas. They are the ones that will help you make more sense of the material. You can turn those trigger words into questions for maximum benefit. How do you identify those key or trigger words? It's easier than you think.

It's easier to find trigger words in nonfiction because the structure is more obvious. It's filled with bold print, titles, headings, and other attention getters. When previewing fiction, such as short stories, plays, novels, and poetry, you'll find trigger words in the names of persons, places, and things. Or, sometimes, they are found in repetition or the location of a word.

When you read a book, magazine, or other publication, scan it quickly. The structure provides you with the clues to use for asking questions. Basically, everything that is out of the ordinary gives you the content for a potential question. All you need to add are the questioning words: "why, what, who, how, where, and when."

As you scan for trigger words or key words, you'll discover an urge to focus on the particulars, the details.

Simply let that urge go, and return to high-speed scanning, taking about two to ten seconds per page. If you start reading for details too soon, you could easily end up slowing down and plodding through paragraphs and pages that have no relevance to your purpose. That could lead to a loss of momentum. To avoid this, keep the book at a greater distance from you than you're used to and hold back on all the details.

Go quickly through the material to locate or discover anything that prompts your brain for a question. The possibilities include:

- Anything with bullets
- Anything with titles
- All the subtitles
- Table of contents
- Headings
- Subheadings
- Front and back covers
- First and last pages of books
- Copyright date
- Index
- Text in boldface
- Italic print
- First and last paragraphs of any sections
- Sections and material in boxes
- Any figures or charts
- Chapter summaries

– Previews or review questions

– Anything that catches your attention

As an example, if the title is, "The Twenty-first Century's Most Dangerous Epidemic," your questions are likely, "What is it?" "Who identified it?" "How bad is it?" "Where is it happening?" "Who is affected by it?" "What's next?" Every single piece of data can be turned into a question. Questions are far more powerful than answers.

You might say, "But I need answers, not just another bunch of questions." Yet, at this stage of your progress with the material, the questions will do more for you, in the long run, than the answers. Questions will give your brain a goal, so it can go into a search-and-find mode. Questions continue to be processed on many levels long after you've found an answer. Questions stimulate thinking; answers don't.

You'll learn a great deal by scanning and asking questions. It seems as if it's not useful for real learning, but it is. You'll learn three types of information:

1. Key content ideas,

2. the basic structure of the material, and

3. thousands of words, ideas, or meanings that were picked up subconsciously, through your peripheral vision.

At times, you will literally find everything you want to know, just through this scanning process. That's one of the unexpected joys of prereading. You'll learn what to expect, where to look for important information. In time, this step will become the most valued part of your overall reading process.

Alter your strategy through prereading.
The whole point of prereading is to gain enough information to decide upon a new course of action. If you go through all the time and work to preread, you'll have laid the foundation for efficient learning.

At this point, you might ask yourself such critical questions as, "Is reading the entire document relevant or necessary to my purpose?" Or, "Could I gain what I want by reading a single chapter or section instead?" Or, "How much time can I commit to satisfy my purpose?" Or, "Do I need just a basic understanding or do I need specific details?" You may also ask yourself, "Do I want to study something in depth, or just enjoy it for passing the time or relaxation?"

Many students and businesspeople complain about massive materials they encounter, such as texts, specification manuals, stacks of computer printouts, technical manuals, journals, and software manuals. Yet their eyes light up with pleasure and amazement when using the prereading skills you're now learning. Reading stacks of school, business, or teacher-generated papers is simple when you use the prereading process.

Now is the time in the prereading process for you to make a specific time commitment. It will put your attention on the task at hand. Now is also the time for you to adjust your strategies. Do you read all or part of the material? Do you take notes or not? Do you use a highlighter or not? Do you read just a few pages or not? This is the time to make specific and relevant decisions about the reading you're about to do. No longer are you an open-to-the-first-page-and-go type of reader. You're savvy and sharp.

You choose what to read, how to read it, and what to do with what you read. And that skill feels good! Remember, this is an active process. Feel free to take some notes while you find questions to ask—nothing extensive, just whatever jumps into your mind as important. But do make sure that you copy onto your notes the chapter titles, each of the subtitles, and the main ideas. This will take only a few seconds a page, but it will give you important clues to the material and help you to read it faster later on because you will be prepared for new ideas.

Look over the visual aids, such as maps, charts, diagrams, illustrations, and pictures. They will help you grasp each point quickly. Then read any summaries or questions at the end of the chapter. Summaries usually are helpful because they include the points the author felt to be most important.

Now, before proceeding with your study, set two goals. Set a *comprehension goal*; decide how well you need to know the material. Will you be tested? If so, how thoroughly? Set a *time goal* for your particular section or chapter based upon how well you need to know it. Is it easy or familiar material? Your goal may be 15 pages an hour but whatever your goal, make sure that it is only for one chapter or section—setting lengthy or unrealistic goals only leads to discouragement and failure. By achieving both of these goals—comprehension and time—you will greatly speed up your study time. At this stage you should have in your notes the chapter title, subtitles, and all major ideas. You should already know a lot about the material—and you haven't even read it yet!

Gather Answers

So far, you've made two passes at the material. It took some time, but it was well worth it. You figured out the overall pattern to your material, then you primed your mind for gathering the rich information and meaning you want. In short, you've gotten yourself ready to read fast and with high comprehension. In fact, if you already think you have a feel for the material, great! That's exactly what you want to have. If you still feel unsure about the material, that's fine, too. You're about to get a good opportunity now to make up some real ground in the comprehension department.

Now is the time to get focused. It is the time to get the answers to the questions you've been posing to your mind. Read the chapter as quickly as you can to understand the ideas. After each page or major idea, go back to your notes and add the supporting details to them. Read no more than one page without writing something down. This is an important key to textbook comprehension and retention. Respond to the material by continually summarizing it in your notes, using your own words.

The old way of studying was to read and forget. Get into the habit of *reading and responding.* You will find even the most boring books become interesting. Avoid using highlighter, magic marker, or felt-tip pens. It's too early to decide what is most important until you've read the entire chapter, it postpones learning, and you might just end up with an expensive coloring book! Remember, coloring is not learning.

Instead, use a pencil to mark important ideas. Whenever something looks valuable, put a checkmark in the margin, next to the passage. It marks what is important, but is not permanent. Later on, during a review, you can reevaluate your marks and either leave them in place, erase them, or add a second one for emphasis. This system is one of the most valuable tools you can use. Not only is it flexible, but it is inexpensive. Continue reading each chapter, or section, marking what is important with a check, and adding to your notes until you are finished.

Evaluate and Respond

Are you still with us? Hang in there, we have just a bit more to go. Your mind is beginning to learn the information in a far better way than the old way of stare and hope. This is a much more active process and, although it takes time and energy, it's well worth it. Let's figure out what we have, and what we don't. Use this as a quick mental checklist:

- Go back to the beginning of your material and browse through it quickly to refresh your memory.
- Answer the chapter question provided by the author.
- Answer the questions you asked.
- What are the key relationships?
- Can you talk about each chapter title, topic, and subtopic you studied from the table of contents?
- Do you now have mental details to support each main idea?
- Can you study that chapter from your notes?

When you get used to being able to know those types of questions and answers, you'll be a more complete (and successful) learner. Why? Part of succeeding at learning is to know what you don't know and to know what questions to ask. Your goal so far has been to get the key meaning, the key concepts, and the key material out of the text into your notes (via your mind). That can be done with any subject. Here is an example of math notes by math tutor and master teacher Geoff Peterson from New Zealand.

Textbooks written by scientists, professors, or technical writers can be wordy and difficult to understand—but *that* you can deal with easily. Put the ideas in your own words or visual diagrams and you will learn the material much faster. You may also want to consider what conclusions (if any) the author draws. Do you agree with them? Why did the author come to those con-

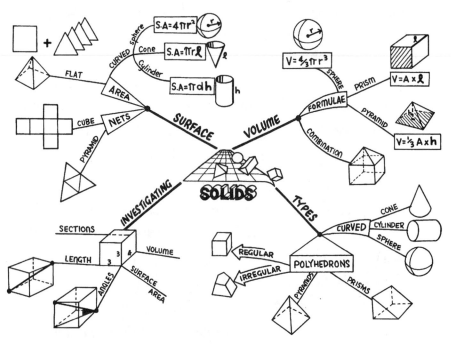

FIGURE 4-2

clusions? If you do not agree, in what areas was the author weak? Were his or her premises weak or only his or her conclusions? These are designed just to get you engaged in the material in some of the same ways the author is thinking.

MAKING MEANING

Meaning is a critical part of the whole learning process. If you're like many students, you're drowning in information and starved for meaning. Yet, many teachers assume that students will automatically find learning meaningful. They don't. What's especially interesting is how meaning mediates our representations of things. How we *feel* about *what* we learn, *changes how we perceive it.* Our mind first evaluates things on a good-bad continuum. Then it's weighed in terms of potency (impact, size, power) and, finally, the activity criteria (movement, warmth, excitement). If you think a political leader is fairly effective, but has low power and is boring, the influence the leader generates may be low.

The search for meaning is innate. You are trying to make sense out of what is happening at all times. Sometimes you need time to go internal and create individual meaning for what you learn. But, while the search for meaning is natural, the success of the search is often left to chance. Nothing has meaning unless you give it your meaning. It's either meaningless information or the meaning is developed, assigned, or created by your mind. But what is this mysterious or elusive process? Our brain craves meaning and the quest for it causes us to find any pattern we can from information. A funny thing about the brain is that it craves meaning so much that what information is lacking in a pattern, it makes up.

As an example:

Let's say you go out to a restaurant. Another couple enters the restaurant, waiting to be seated. You know them; they are married, but not to each other. Suddenly, in the absence of information, your brain immediately begins constructing reasons, scenarios, and models of understanding. You ask yourself, "Didn't I see those two together last week at a meeting? Didn't they both volunteer to work on the same organizing committee?" What the brain isn't given, it makes up (and it might be wrong!).

There are three primary ways you make something meaningful. These may not be *purposely* done by you, but nonetheless, they are still done. These are:

1. Relevance.
2. Emotions.
3. Pattern-making.

Any of these three are going to trigger some meaning for you. Two or three out of three will create a much stronger sense of meaning.

Relevance. What you have seen or heard before gets processed differently and faster by your brain. What you relate to personally, you'll understand better. What you have prior hooks for, you'll make more sense out of. The value of this for creating meaning is simple. You've created the mental magnets so that when you see them again later, they will be more familiar to you. What you have background knowledge on, you can read faster. In reading, you can create more relevance several ways.

WHAT TO DO NOW

One of the best ways to improve your speed is to read something more basic, more simple, more juvenile on the same topic. That gives you the vocabulary, the hooks, and the background to make more of what you read relevant. Another strategy is to preread the material (see pages 108–111). As we discussed, prereading is to browse through the material very quickly, generally about one to five seconds a page. It works because, at this pace, instead of reading, you can be creating connections, establishing your purpose, asking relevant questions, and mapping out the organizational structure and main themes of the book.

Now, can you relate the text material to class lecture notes? If not, can you now invest time to integrate and remember your material? It is as important as reading it. If your notes are unclear, try rewriting them, basing your organization around the main ideas. Think about the concepts presented in the chapter and try to explain them in your own words.

• • • • • • • • • • • • • •

Engage emotions. Read something frightening, sad, joyful, suspenseful, horrible, sexy, or provocative. The experience affects your sensory system and your mind reacts with an emotional response. When your emotions are engaged, the brain codes the content you're reading by triggering the release of chemicals that single out and mark the experience as important and meaningful.

A mild emotion may give meaning to something without your having any understanding of it. Your brain can also give meaning to something you hate. It's simply an automatic chemical process—you experience emotions and it will become meaningful.

In reading, you can take advantage of this phenomenon. The stronger you feel about something you read, the more likely you are to remember it and make sense out of it. The good thing about this is that it works both ways; hating something or disagreeing with something works just as well as liking something or strongly agreeing with it.

```
┌─────────────────────────────────────────────┐
│            WHAT TO DO NOW                     │
└─────────────────────────────────────────────┘
```

As you read, stop occasionally to consider how you feel about what you read. The worst reaction is no reaction. Pause and simply allow the feelings you are having to intensify. You can talk out loud about what you read to let the attitude build stronger. Create feelings, argue with someone else about the topic, act it out, or debate it. The more intense the feelings, the more meaningful the topic becomes.

• • • • • • • • • • • • • •

Pattern-making. Once you grasp the overall big picture, all the remaining pieces will have a lot more meaning. As we said before, a jigsaw puzzle is much easier to complete if you know what the finished picture is supposed to look like. Hold up the right piece, see the cover of the puzzle solution, and locate where the piece fits in. This can be one form of the grand A-ha! experience—or that moment could come later, over quiet reflection, on a walk, or in the shower.

That's why, without a preview in reading, you might find yourself thinking, "Where is the author going with this? How does this fit in?" You may not know the answer until you have gone much of the way through the book. The overview is like receiving a map to a new city in which you've just arrived. Once you have the map, you can move around more comfortably. But how do you get this map?

WHAT TO DO NOW

Earlier in this chapter, on page 74, you saw an example of a structural map of the material. Before you read anything longer than a magazine or newspaper, take the time to make one. The maps are simply a visual representation of what you think the material will be about. Below, are some examples of what other students have done:

• • • • • • • • • • • • •

– Practice recalling information with and without your notes.

– Learn to study and reflect as much as possible from your notes. They are bound to be more understandable than the text.

– Avoid rereading and rereading your texts. It is best to only browse through them from now on and ask or look for questions and answers.

FROM SHORT- TO LONG-TERM LEARNING

There are many ways to transfer learning from short-term to long-term memory. The single most critical ingredient is to process the learning—do something with it. It's a poor use of your time to read something and forget it. You're just too busy and the stakes are too high. If it's worth learning, make it worth recalling. There's a whole chapter coming up (Chapter 8) on tips to embed what you learn in long-term memory. But here are some specific tips:

- Attach a strong emotion to the material.
- Repeat and review the material within 10 minutes, 48 hours, and 7 days.
- Make a concrete reminder—a token or artifact such as a political button.
- Act out the material or do a fun role play in your own room.
- Put it on a picture or poster—use intense colors.
- Summarize on paper and words in your notes.
- Review in different senses, using aromas, for example.
- Implement and really use the material in your own personal life.
- Make a simple video or audiotape.
- Download your material to your computer for later review.
- Use mnemonics/acronyms.

- Create or redo a song; make a rap.
- Make and tell a story about the material.
- Use real situations for practice in learning if possible.
- Hold an unguided discussion with a peer on the material.
- Follow up the learning with your journal writing.
- Build a working model of what you learned. (Use clay, foam, or paper cut-outs.)
- Find a buddy-support group.
- Put the material into smaller groups of three, four, or seven.

The use of these tools, which we'll explore in more detail in later chapters, will be one of your most worthwhile investments. Remember, it's not what you know, it's whether you know it in the right context when you really need it. Most likely, your exams are a test of your thinking, writing, and recalling abilities, not usually just your reading skills. So practice *thinking*, practice *writing*, and practice *recalling* your notes and the text material. The study process you have just learned emphasizes organization and recall. It is simple, yet effective. Let's review the parts.

Review These Points

**Study by P-A-G-E—Prepare, Ask,
Gather, and Evaluate**
Prepare Your Mind
Ask Questions
Gather Answers
Evaluate and Respond

Making Meaning

From Short- to Long-Term Learning

5

READING FOR RESULTS:

How to Have It All—Speed and Comprehension

Because you've come this far, it's safe to say you can read. Millions of people can't read, and life is a constant terror. They can't follow simple printed directions; they may get lost at malls, airports, highways, and in buildings. They can't read signs; they can't do comparison shopping; they can't read a prescription label or enjoy many TV shows. They can't enjoy a good book. They can't fill out a simple form, from a driver's license test to a job application. Life can be pretty grim when you can't read. So if you *can* read, take advantage of it!

READING FOR SPEED

This chapter is designed to help you become good at reading so that, even if you still dislike some of your texts, at least you'll be able to dislike them for less time. This first section is on rapid reading—an essential for success in school. Most students with poor grades need help in reading skills. Yet, it's no wonder—their last reading lesson may have been in the second grade, and it's unlikely anyone has had a class in comprehension or speed since then. High-powered reading skills can help make school more enjoyable and create plenty of free time. Let's get started.

Positive Mindset

Would it help you if you could read twice as fast as you do now? If that sounds impossible, it's not. The human mind is capable of seeing and understanding material nearly as fast as one can turn pages. Surprisingly, many people have, and can now still read that fast. The famous English philosopher John Stuart Mill read a page in five seconds. So did presidents Teddy Roosevelt and John F. Kennedy. If others did it, why can't you? No one knows our upper limits in reading. Here are some factors that may influence your reading rate:

The material itself. Is it small or large print? Are there pictures? Is it clear, easy to read? Is it written by a good writer?

Your needs. How well do you need to know the material? Do you need just a general sense of it? Or, do you need a very detailed understanding and analysis of it? How well you need to know it changes your approach and your rate.

Your personal background in the material. Often, a scientist can read a science book faster than a non-scientist, since the text probably requires some kind of content background.

The circumstances. How alert or awake are you? How is the lighting, the amount of fresh air? Are you alert or tired? What kind of desk or chair do you have?

The limiters listed above can be dealt with and their impact minimized. It takes some time, but it can be done. A book alone cannot give the same kind of help that is necessary to make a dramatic increase in your reading skills. The ideal is to get some professional help from a well-trained rapid-reading instructor. But, in the meantime, there *are* some positive steps you can take.

Now, before you start, remember those fast readers we mentioned earlier? Fast readers were fast *not* because they were born that way. They *learned* to read fast. How? They did certain things right. How do we know? Success leaves clues! Here are some of the things they did:

Set Focusing Goals

Why set goals, even if you're not sure you can reach them? Simple. Goals focus the mind. They allow you to discard all other ideas, options, and strategies until you do what you set out to do. The more you are committed to your goals, the more likely you are to reach them. Start with an attitude that you *can* succeed. Commit yourself to being able to succeed. Never question whether it can be done. Make it not a question of *how*, but a question of *when*.

Both short- and long-term goals are important. The short-term is usually for the next few minutes or hours. What do you want to do tonight? Write out your goals on a Post-it and put it right in front of you. Your long-term goals are important, too. Those can be for this term at school, for your whole education, or even life goals. Sometimes you'll invest more in your short-term, and other times, more in your long-term goals. You'll find the balance.

Use "Lazy Eyes"

As children, we were generally taught the *look-say* method—look at a word, then say it. So, we learn to say words to ourselves. That can slow us down, and, sometimes lead to boredom. That drops concentration, so the comprehension and speed drops, too. It's a vicious circle.

Students often say, "I can't read fast; I have too many bad habits!" It's true there are some bad habits that slow one's reading. It's also true that you have the ability to understand those habits and to build new, better habits. What are some of those poor habits you'll want to understand?

They include:

— Subvocalization (pronouncing words to yourself)

— Regression (going back to reread material already covered)

— Prolonged fixation (stopping and staring at one word)

— Inefficient eye movement (losing your place and wandering between lines)

These poor habits cause tired eyes, boredom, low reading speeds, and low comprehension.

It is not ability that you lack; it's training. Because we are taught to read at 100 to 300 words per minute, we are led to believe that is our normal rate. But your mind actually gets bored when you go too slowly. Each type of material has a peak rate at which you can read, based primarily on your background in that subject. But now that you know the words, and how they are pronounced, you can skim over them quicker with lazy eyes, instead of scrutinizing each word, as if it is the secret to the universe.

Learn to see
the area at the top of this
particular box

Then you can easily see the
area in the middle of this.

Your eyes can now learn,
with time, to move
vertically to see the lower
area of this box. Wow!

FIGURE 5-1

Lazy eyes are when your eyes look over an *area,* on the page, instead of just a word. This prevents unnecessary backing up and rereading, which consumes about one sixth of your reading time. It also prevents unneeded prolonged fixations—the habit of staring at one word or phrase for a long period. In other words, it's OK if your eyes are a bit lazy and look at bigger groups of words instead of individual words.

Your reading focus is different from your usual vision. The difference is easy to explain. What do you see when you look outside your window? Do your eyes focus only on a spot three-quarters of an inch by five-eighths of an inch? What you see is an entire panorama with everything in focus. You should see a page in the same way. In order to regain your usual range of vision for reading, you will need some practice.

STOP AND TAKE ACTION

This will require the use of both hands and a large book.

◆ Flip through the pages of the book quickly, turning them from the top with your left hand and pulling your eyes down the page by brushing down each page with the edge of your right hand. Your fingers should be extended and relaxed.

◆ Follow your hand down each page with your eyes, trying to see as many words as possible.

◆ Start by drifting down each page in two or three seconds, gradually reducing the time spent on each page until you can go as fast as you can turn pages.

◆ Pace yourself, starting at 20 pages a minute, slowly increasing to 100 pages a minute within one to two months. This practice work helps your eyes see more words at a time by preventing zooming in or focusing only on individual words.

◆ Practice for five minutes a day for several weeks.

Remember that you'll read faster with practice than without it. Reading is a skill, and, as with any skill, all the instruction in the world won't help you unless you actually practice what you learn. It's important to learn to see more words at a time. Just those few minutes a day of practice will help keep you from missing words.

You might be concerned that if you go faster, you'll miss words. But you already know most of the words you're about to see. There are more than 600,000 words in our language, but 400 of them comprise 65 percent of the printed material. These are structure words that have no meaning, but they tie the sentence together. For example, in the second sentence of this paragraph, the structure words are: *but, of, the, to.* Remove most of those words and the sentence is choppy, but still readable: "you already know most words you see." Because you've read those 400 words many times, don't let them slow down your reading by dwelling on them. Remember, proper practice, proper practice, and you get perfect (or almost).

Adjust Your Rates

Does everything mean the same? Is everything at the same level of difficulty? Do you have the same background in all subjects? The same interest? Of course not. Learn to read different things at different rates.

As an example, you might read light fiction quickly and technical texts at about one half that rate. When you read easy material, speed up and you will enjoy reading more. A common misconception is that reading faster ruins enjoyment. That is not true. When you were in first grade, you probably read at a rate of 10 to 30 words per minute. Now you may read 100 to 300 words per minute—a full ten times faster! Did you lose any of the enjoyment of books? Of course not, and in fact, you may enjoy books more now than when you read slowly.

Magazines can be scanned quickly or read slowly for fun. Textbooks should be done both ways; scan first, then "study read." Decide upon your purpose and read to seek the level of comprehension you require. When your purpose in reading is entertainment, read faster than usual. In a high accountability situation (a tough test), read at your maximum rate of comprehension (that may or may not be fast) but not to memorize. Make the recalling of your material a separate step later on.

Read with an Attitude

Attitude is important. The best attitude is total confidence. Do you see yourself as a slow reader or a fast reader? Your actions are consistent with your conception of yourself. Always push yourself, being aware of what you need to get out of the material. Believe you can get what you want, when you want it. Research has suggested that what we think about ourselves often comes true. We think of ourselves many times during the day, but let's talk about reading. When you think about having to read, what do you say to yourself? Is it, "I am so slow; I hate to read!" Or, do you say to yourself, "Reading is cool; I hope I can blast through my assignment pretty quickly tonight." What you say to yourself may, in fact, affect *how* you read when you start.

Science and the Olympic athletes have popularized the concept of mental practice, and thousands have used it successfully. Our minds may have a goal-striving mechanism that simply needs to be triggered properly in order to automatically steer us toward a set goal. What does this mean to you in practical terms? It means that you can program yourself to become a better reader, or anything else you like, by using a beautiful built-in success mechanism. This success mechanism is a goal-directed instinct that is easily motivated. In fact, you can learn to become a better reader without even reading a book (though reading *does* help a lot!).

First, make sure the goal you seek is realistic and desirable; otherwise, your internal mechanism may not get the clear signal it needs. Get a strong, clear, and vivid picture of yourself achieving the role you want. If it's reading improvement you want, sit back, close your eyes, and picture yourself sitting down at a desk or table you're comfortable with, moving down the page, not only comprehending what you have read, but quickly recalling it in your notes. Practice this once or twice a day for about two minutes each time. Within several weeks, you should see a noticeable improvement in yourself.

Practice Reading Fast

Practice does not make perfect; practice only makes permanent. If you want to be a good reader, *you have to read fast to get good at reading fast.* Practice and use your skills on everything. Read magazines, read novels, read newspapers, read letters. Reading is a skill and doing more of it keeps your skills sharp.

If you get tired easily and your eyes seem to wear out, consider two options. One, have your eyes checked; you may need glasses or contacts. If you already have them, you may need to change the prescription. There is one other hint that may help you read fast. It is often overlooked, but so simple: Change the distance of the material from your eyes. Hold your book four to six inches further away from your eyes than usual. Your eyes won't have to work so hard because the further things are from your eyes, the less movement it takes to see everything. So be sure your material is at least 15 inches from your eyes; you'll enjoy increased speed and comprehension, and reduce fatigue.

READING FOR COMPREHENSION

There's been such a mystery among most students about what brings understanding home. But there's really no secret to it. Comprehension is a set of skills that include concentration, decoding, and having relevant background for understanding. Let's explore some of the key ingredients in detail.

Use Background Material

Background is the reason why a beginning law student might read at 70 to 200 words per minute, yet a practicing attorney can read the same material much faster. The background gives you the vocabulary, the associations, and the experience to more easily comprehend the material. Sometimes a good way to better understand something is to learn about it from other sources before you read.

It's easy to learn to gain the necessary background for a subject. Excellent ways to accomplish this are:

1. reading other material on that subject
2. personal experience
3. listening to lectures
4. prereading the material earlier and reading other easier material on the same subject. The purpose of prereading is to become familiar with the main ideas and to organize those ideas into a pattern. This organizing step is crucial in developing speed in reading textbook material.

Become an Active Reader

Reading is an active process, not a passive one. Anticipate ideas and read for a purpose to answer your questions by actively searching for the information you want. Have questions in mind before you read, not afterwards. If you begin reading a book with questions, you'll complete your reading with the answers. Think about important points and read to understand them. Be confident that you can get what you want and you will. Don't argue with the author while reading. Save critical analysis for later so you will not slow yourself down, lose concentration, and miss the flow of the material. Put a pencil check in the margin of areas you would like to go back to.

How do you gain meaning from the material? In the last chapter, we suggested three things: relevance, patterns, and emotions. As a reminder, you can help your mind make more meaning:

1. By making associations of personal relevance. The more you can relate to the material, the more the meaning.

2. You can help insure that the more the information fits in a larger pattern, the more sense it will make. It's a bit like a jigsaw puzzle. The individual puzzle piece means very little by itself. But when you put the other pieces around it, it starts to make much more sense. This means that when you are reading, make sure you know the context, the related ideas, and where it all fits in. To do that, make a mind map of the material like the ones illustrated in the last chapter.

3. The more emotional response the material evokes, the more meaning. Feel deeply about it; love or hate is better than no feelings at all.

As an example:

To illustrate these points, let's take the September 11, 2001, terrorist attacks on America. Did it have any relevance (1) to you? If you knew any of the victims or someone who was close to them or anyone who was part of the emergency teams, it had stronger relevance. Was there meaning to the pattern (2)? Was this part of a larger pattern of global anti-American terrorism? Was it part of a failed string of CIA or FBI investigations? Is it part of the changing

**You have a lot to do with how
your studying turns out.**

landscape of crime in the world? Was it the loss of our innocence as a global power? Did the media portray it as part of a wider pattern of anti-Americanism? Finally, did it evoke a strong emotion (3)? Yes, it did, and the emotion was stronger the closer you got to the event. This is an example of how we create meaning: relevance, patterns, and emotion.

But how can you use this information to help you understand your learning better? Certainly the more meaning, the more interesting and stronger the memory. The answer is simple. It will take active learning on your part to make most of your learning meaningful.

Read to Understand, Not Just to Memorize

In order to have a smooth, continuous flow of information to your mind, don't stop to memorize facts. Save that process for later when you study your notes. Read a page, summarize the data in your notes, then continue. At all times you should read as rapidly as you can understand the ideas. Let your notes save the ideas for later on. It's okay to read something and not recall it a minute later.

Actually, your brain is better designed to recall pictures, graphics, and illustrations than text material. So, take advantage of that. Draw out what you learn. Make patterns, doodles, and drawings. You'll remember it more by being active and creating meaning out of what you read than by slowing it down and hoping it will somehow sink in.

Keep a Hungry Attitude

Get into a focused, hungry-learn reading state. You might say to yourself, "Once I get this reading done, I'll be able to go do something I enjoy more." Don't use negative reinforcement or a self-threat such as, "If I don't get an A in this class, I'll lose my scholarship." If you maintain a strong, receptive attitude, you will find comprehension will be easier because you are not fighting yourself. Fighting reading is much like panicking while swimming. The secret is to relax and go with the content.

How do you keep a hungry attitude? Many students find that it helps to have some kind of a reminder, right on your desk. A friend of mine always studies with his wristwatch laid next to his book. Others might like a stopwatch. You might study in three-minute segments, so you get a sands-of-time hourglass. Put something on your desk to keep you focused and on task.

Maintain the Body Edge

It's difficult to comprehend what you read when you are tired, sleepy, depressed, or in pain. Some students complain that their comprehension is poor while doing their reading at three in the morning. At that hour, many couldn't comprehend a fortune cookie! It is critical not only to be alert, but relaxed. Be comfortable and in tune with the subject of the book.

Reading posture definitely affects comprehension. Sit at a desk when possible. Study in an upright position with the book flat on the table, 15 or more inches away.

The more stretched out and relaxed your study position, the more you will encourage its usual result—drowsiness, poor concentration, or sleep. If you want comprehension, speed, and retention, sit up alertly, and act as though you are serious about accomplishing the task.

The body edge also means taking care of other related things. Does your chair provide the right angle for reading and comfort? Are you eating the right foods for learning? As we discussed in Chapter 2, this means proteins, fructose, and complex, not simple carbohydrates. Eat your lean meats, cheese, nuts, yogurt, fruits, and dark green vegetables. Make sure your lighting is good. You'll want natural or incandescent lighting, if possible. Have a glass of pure water near you to prevent dehydration. Wear comfortable, loose clothing and make sure the sound level is good for your concentration.

Master the Preread

The whole concept of prereading (see Chapter 4) leaves many readers discouraged or skeptical of speed-reading. They often feel it's just too much extra work. Let's address those concerns. Here are some of the comments often made about prereading and the real story behind them.

Myth: Prereading is too much work.
Reality: Prereading saves time.

Think of your reading requirements as not how many minutes or seconds per page, but how much time per project. While a traditional slower reader may formally read something over once, they'll often make the time to go back to reread something they missed again and again. That rereading is dismissed as: "Of course you go back; you need to." What counts is this: "Is the total time, from start to finish any less for you to get what you needed out of your reading?" With prereading, the answer is usually yes.

Myth: Prereading is something new.
Reality: You've used the concept many times.

Prereading allows your mind to do several things:

1. Get a mental map of the material before reading it.

2. Discover what you know and don't know ahead of time.

3. Plant some seeds for new ideas.

4. Find your way around the material faster.

5. Better understand what you're being exposed to.

6. Help you figure out what you want to know.

7. Feel more confident about what you're learning through repetition.

Have you used this concept before? Many times, and in many other areas of your life. Here are just a few of many possible examples:

1. Movies. Before you see a movie, you've often heard or seen previews of it or talked to others who've seen it.

2. Visiting friends. Before you go to someone's house for the first time, you often look over a map or the directions, or ask others how to get there.

3. Shopping. Before you purchase something, you've often heard about the item or seen it advertised, you've seen the product used, or you've browsed through stores or talked to friends who already own that product.

4. Driving a car. You had a tricycle or a bicycle, rode in bumper cars and your parents' cars, saw movies in which people were driving, or played video games related to driving.

In short, a great deal of what you do in life you have "pre-done." That's an important aid in learning. Yet, in spite of how valuable prereading is, there are times when you don't want to preread. Those times include reading a letter from a friend, a suspenseful or dramatic novel, or poetry. But for the vast majority of your reading, you'll want to do the prereading process.

Myth: Prereading is a big waste of time.
Reality: It's more aligned with the way your brain is designed to learn.

We can only read what we already know. That is, the human brain can only comprehend patterns that are familiar. The more you know about a text before you actually read it, the easier it will be to read. Your brain works better with small, bite-sized chunks. We make sense out of ideas that we have heard before, not wild, out-of-the-blue ideas. The design of the human brain is such that it does poorly in learning big, new, or fresh ideas.

Have you ever tried to explain a big new idea or novel concept to friends? It's tough! They usually listen, then when you're done, say something like, "Well, I'm sure it's a good idea, but I just don't get it. But you can go ahead. Keep me posted." Perhaps their brain just doesn't have the existing connections or networks to create any meaning out of it. The real secret to preparing the brain for better comprehension, meaning, and recall at a high rate is prereading. It provides the patterns, the hooks, the vocabulary, the map, the questions, and the overview that make for better reading. Prereading is simple and critical to your success.

Thus, creating a reading purpose and time management are inseparable. In the information age, we can no longer presume to read every document at the same speed or level of comprehension. Not only is this impossible, but with the amount of material we need to read, it is not even desirable.

Prereading has an added advantage. It promotes long-term memory because of repetition. It helps you comprehend and categorize the material you read. It encourages you to build a mental structure of what you read. Any material you actively organize, you will remember longer.

Formulate a Purpose

You'll want to be sure to establish your purpose every time you read. A purpose is the *why* you are reading. It's not well defined as a goal ("I'll finish these 20 pages by 9:00 tonight."). It's much more vague, such as, "I want to learn what this has to do with my life." Or, I want a general understanding of this topic." When you establish your purpose, the real power of your brain comes immediately into play.

As a nice fringe benefit, creating a purpose releases the long-time vice-grip of guilt. You know the kind—the kind that happens when you violate those old rules about how we are "supposed" to read. It usually takes the form of, "I bought this magazine, so even if I don't *want* to read all the articles, I ought to—otherwise, I wasted my money!"

With a better sense of purpose, you can justify putting aside the material you do not need to read. You'll be better able to throw out, reassess, or give away those publications that waste your valuable time.

Establishing a prereading purpose takes as little as five seconds. But over the course of a lifetime, the savings to you in time, guilt, and convenience can be huge. This simple strategy is so critical and far-reaching that it can instantly and permanently change your relationship and results in reading.

When we clarify our study purpose, we greatly increase our odds of accomplishing it. Purpose focuses energy and attention. Give your mind a clear focus and purpose, and almost anything can be accomplished. In fact, your purpose is the driving force behind all reading.

Here's why it's critical. Francis Bacon, the great English philosopher, said, "Some books are to be tasted, others to be swallowed, and some few to be chewed and digested; that is, some books are to be read only in parts, others to be read but not curiously; and some few to be read wholly, and with diligence and attention."

In short, your purpose is so different from one reading material to the next that it can totally change your strategy for that material. Examples of diversity in purpose include:

For a magazine: *Build on areas of interest.* Add something new. Find all articles that relate to your interests. Recall needed: Low to moderate. Pleasure desired: Moderate to high. End product: Highlight key ideas or tear them out and enter into your "to do" list.

For a distraction only: *Your purpose could be non-productive.* For instance, your main purpose for reading in the doctor's waiting room may be to occupy your time, simply a distraction. That can be, at times, just as legitimate a purpose as reading for a test you have to pass.

For a newspaper: *The broad update.* Get a quick update on local, national, and international stories. Enjoy your favorite comics. Check local TV listings. Read any interesting people or sports stories. Recall needed: Low. Pleasure desired: Moderate. End product: Learn just enough to feel that you are "keeping up with the important stories and with friends and colleagues."

For a textbook: *Become detail-literate.* Get a solid background in both the overview and the specifics. Read on several levels. Recall needed: Moderate to high. Pleasure desired: Irrelevant. End product: Learn enough to be able to write about it, converse on it, and pass tests on it.

In summary, go about your reading with a great sense of value about your own time. You can waste money, but you can always replace money. Your time is the most valuable and, in fact, the only thing you have. If you don't get value from what you're reading, you are wasting your time. The best time to practice these tips is on the very next thing you have to read. How about giving it a try?

Organize What You Read

Your mind seeks organization, logical sequences, and order. Give it a chance to comprehend the material by grouping ideas and details into meaningful blocks. Restructure the material into easy-to-picture thoughts. Use every possible combination of thought-pictures that will work. When you perceive the unity and structure of the material you are studying, you will grasp its meaning much faster. Strive toward understanding the structure as well as the details. Here's an example of organizing what is being read *while* it's being read. The format is a schematic or graphic organizer. If I were studying first-year neurophysiology in college, my preliminary overview of the textbook might look like this:

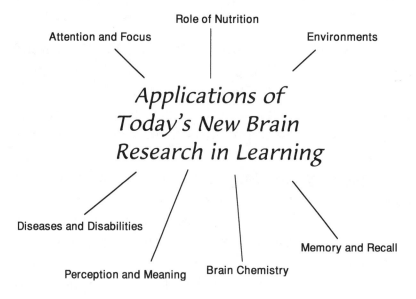

Role of Nutrition

Attention and Focus

Environments

Applications of Today's New Brain Research in Learning

Diseases and Disabilities

Perception and Meaning

Brain Chemistry

Memory and Recall

FIGURE 5-2

Write as You Read

Get in the habit of recalling on paper immediately what you have read. Because you will better understand each point, the following point will be that much clearer. Comprehension depends upon understanding each preceding idea. The better you understand and recall them, the more likely you will understand the next.

As we have discussed, one of the ways to write as you read is to use graphic organizers and mind maps. Use patterns like a spider web, spokes of a wheel, and road maps. Place key ideas in the center and let the other ideas branch out. Figure 5-2 will help you get some ideas. Stick to each part of the study process and you will find comprehension becoming a habit.

Read Quickly and in a Focused Way

Readers with the best comprehension are usually fast readers. The slower you read, the more chances there are for you to daydream and lose concentration, hence, comprehension. Good comprehension is a process and a habit, not a mystery. Comprehension is largely dependent on how well you already know the subject. Because background increases vocabulary and subject familiarity, get the most amount of prior knowledge you can. Processing then becomes almost subliminal, it happens so fast. When you have an extensive background, there is even a point at which material can be read prior to conscious awareness.

ACCOUNTABILITY—USE IT!

Make yourself use what you read. Find ways to apply something from it; even just talking to one of your parents about it helps. Share what you read with others. Often, good readers have talked about the material with others and have used the learning in their work. In other words, good readers make themselves take advantage of what they read.

All of the strategies will work for you if you work with them. Many students find the best way to integrate them into their reading habits is with 3" × 5" index cards. Put one of each of the ideas on an index card. Either carry the cards with you for constant review or pick one card a week and use it until it becomes a habit. Over time, you'll become a spoiled reader—spoiled for speed and comprehension!

Review These Points

Reading for Speed
Positive Mindset
Set Focusing Goals
Use "Lazy Eyes"
Adjust Your Rates
Read with an Attitude
Practice Reading Fast

Reading for Comprehension
Use Background Material
Become an Active Reader
Read to Understand, Not Just to Memorize
Keep A Hungry Attitude
Maintain the Body Edge
Master the Preread
Formulate a Purpose
Organize What You Read
Write as You Read
Read Quickly and in a Focused Way

Accountability—Use It!

NOTES THAT SPARKLE:
The Kind of Notes You'll Want to Study

LEARN NOTETAKING SKILLS

All of us learn differently and we all have our favorite ways to learn. When students ask what's the best way to study, they should keep in mind that what works for one student may not work for everyone. Some students say notes are a waste of time. The question is, "How are you doing in school?" If you're doing great, maybe your notes are stored in your head. If you could use some help, read on.

Most teachers say strong notes are vital to high grades. Ideally, most of your studying should be done from notes taken in class and from the text. Your notes show how well you understand the material presented. Students are not usually taught how to take concise, creative notes. Most have to learn from others or through trial and error. Soak in the following concepts for general usage. Then use your creativity to develop some formats that work best for you and the subjects in which you are interested.

Summarize, Don't Duplicate

Copy machines are great for making copies. You don't need to be a copy machine. Your notes should not be a duplication but rather a synopsis, a synthesis.

Accuracy is your first consideration. But beyond that, try to reconstruct the material in your own words. That is the beauty of good notes; they are more understandable and interesting than a text or lecture. Study the sample notes at the end of this chapter.

Create Your Own Style

Because you want to avoid having to write out each word, invent some shortcuts. It is time-consuming to spell out each word you choose to include in your notes. You can phonetically abbreviate by using the consonants of a word to create a phonetic representation, which you will be able to write rapidly and interpret easily upon review. Look at the following sentence from a lecture given in a literature class:

Jean-Paul Sartre is a French existentialist who was born in Paris in 1905. (14 words, 75 characters)

You already know Paris is in France (Yes, there are cities with that name around the world, but if it was in an obscure location, you'd say so.) Your notes might read as follows:

Sartre, existnt, Paris 1905. (4 words, 28 characters)

Use as many symbols and abbreviations from math as you can. Figure 6-1 shows some symbols that can be used for shortcuts in notetaking.

Vary Your Print Size

Your attention is attracted to contrast. If everything is the same size and shape, then nothing stands out. But

Symbols for Use in Notetaking

SYMBOL	EXPLANATION
>	greater than, more than
<	less than
=	the same, equals
≠	not the same, different
X	times, cross, trans
→	towards, going
←	from
∴	therefore, because
∞	infinity, a great deal
(+)	positive, good
(-)	negative, against
c̄, w/	with
w/o	without
↓	down, under, decreasing
↑	above, up, increasing
$	dollars, money
Q	question

FIGURE 6-1

if you have something that occasionally stands out, you're more likely to recall it. After all, the thoughts and ideas you record will likely be of varying importance. With some practice, you will begin to automatically write more important ideas in larger size print and less important details in smaller size. Such variations will help you remember your notes more easily, and make them more fun to take down. Another method that is helpful is the use of geometric shapes to identify and categorize ideas. Figure 6-2 shows some examples.

Geometric Key for Use in Notetaking

GEOMETRIC SYMBOL	EXPLANATION
☐	Main Ideas: Inserted in square or Marked with check
√ √	Important Concepts or Facts to Remember: Marked with two checks
⬭	Names of People: Circled
▭	Minor Ideas or Details: Inserted in rectangle
△	Reasons, Why, How: Inserted in triangle
⟶ LETTER SIZE	Relationships or Connecting Ideas: Indicated by arrows and letter size to show subordinate ideas

FIGURE 6-2

Learn Subject Formats

Each subject group has basic characteristics that help you organize information and your thoughts on that particular topic. Many students are stumped in notetaking because in some textbooks the information on each page is not well organized. Some books may have a dozen pages without boldfaced headings or changes in organization. It is often difficult to study and take notes from such textbooks. Fortunately, most textbooks are better written today than they were in the past. Many have chapter summaries, boldfaced headings, and questions to answer. But when you use a book that does not indicate what is important by its format, use the information in Figure 6-3 to help organize your notes and study procedure. Figure 6-3 includes the basic formats for three main subject areas.

In order to take notes well, you must be proficient at sorting information. To understand an idea, you need to see its parts as well as its whole. Depending on the subject, the parts are quite predictable. First, find the main idea; it is often in the first two sentences of each

Basic Subject Formats for Use in Notetaking

SUBJECT AREA	FORMAT AND STRUCTURE
Social Sciences	
Law	Issues and principles
Political Science	Background information
History	Problems, conflicts
Sociology	Reasoning, procedure
Psychology	Decisions, results
	Conclusions, alternatives
Exact Sciences	
Math	Background, idea description
Biology	Laws, theorems, axioms
Physics	Supportive examples, approach
Chemistry	New problems to solve
	Solutions, other applications
Literature	
Novels	Background on author, topic
Plays	Characters
Poetry	Problems, issues defined
	Events, complications
	Crises, problem solved

FIGURE 6-3

paragraph. To do that, look for phrases like *most important, first of all, it must be emphasized that.* Any similar phrase is the author's way of telling you that something important is being said. Second, find supporting details and examples to explain the main idea. These often include stories or data, such as names and dates. Next, isolate the information you will need by sorting actual facts from filler data, such as the author's personal experiences and opinions. This is easy because the facts are often proper names, places, or numbers. Once isolated from the facts, the remaining material can often be identified as filler. Texts often follow a sequence. For example, math texts might follow this sequence: Background information, statement of laws, axioms, or theorems, examples, problems presented to be solved. When you take notes for a math class, don't simply copy an important theorem. Write out examples. Write out pictures, doodles and symbols, *anything* to bring more life out of it. Ensure comprehension by examining the other parts of the sequence of information and making sure you understand it, too.

Use Creative Approaches

The more unusual and eye-catching your notes are, the more likely you will enjoy studying them and be able to recall them. The standard outline form has two major drawbacks—they are inflexible and there is typically great difficulty in recalling them later on. Useful, creative notes take very little practice, but if you need some ideas, refer to Figures 6-4 to 6-11. The whole idea is to make your notes more brain-compatible. That means designing your notes more like the way your brain stores information than by the traditional outline method. Your recall of individual words generally is low.

Your brain stores information as pictures, sounds, and feelings very well. That means, put as much sensory information as possible into your notes and they'll work better for you. Start by thinking of your notes as a creative pattern of connected ideas. Make them similar to a sentence diagram, road map, blueprint, recall pattern, or schematic clustering instead of a list. The purpose of this format is to have clarity and recall. At best, your notes may generate refreshing ideas, great recall, and more creativity. At a minimum, they'll store information and be relaxing and fun. You might use these creative notes for lectures, organizing your thoughts, or studying.

The method to great notes is simple. Take colored pens, and starting in the middle of the paper:

1. Decide on a main topic or idea.
2. Print the topic in the center of your paper and enclose it.
3. Add branches to hold the important points.
4. Add details and key words onto the branches.
5. Add symbols and pictures for better recall. In textbooks, articles, and other nonfiction, the branches could be titled from the boldfaced print or chapter headings, or simply labeled What, How, Why, Who, and When. If there are no clues, make up labels such as purpose, methods, and result. In fiction, use branch labels, such as chapter titles, character names, places, events,

problems, and conclusions. Then attach the details to those branches.

Additional tips: Use pictures, arrows, symbols, cartoons, illustrations, and abbreviations. Put your words on the top of lines; be brief and simple. Turn the paper sideways and use medium to thick colored pens. Printing is more easily recalled than script. Change the size of your words; the more important they are, the bigger they should be made. Use a different color for each of the branches. Be outrageous! Put in action, creativity, and your own personality. Throughout this book, you will find samples. The only element missing—and it's an important one—is color.

Keep Notes Together

An ingenious way to learn a subject quickly and with better understanding is to take notes in tandem. Take class lecture notes on a page opposite the notes you took while studying the text. Ideally, you should read the text and take notes prior to the class lecture. Put your notes on the left-hand side of your paper, leaving the right half for class work (see Figure 6-4).

When the teacher or professor talks, you will not only understand his or her comments better, but you won't have to write as much (See Figure 6-10). If you keep class and text notes on the same topic together on a page, you will take fewer notes and understand more. Other students in class may be writing frantically while you relax and only jot down an occasional supporting detail. Even if you can't take text notes in advance, bring your lecture notes home and reverse the process.

Sample Notes

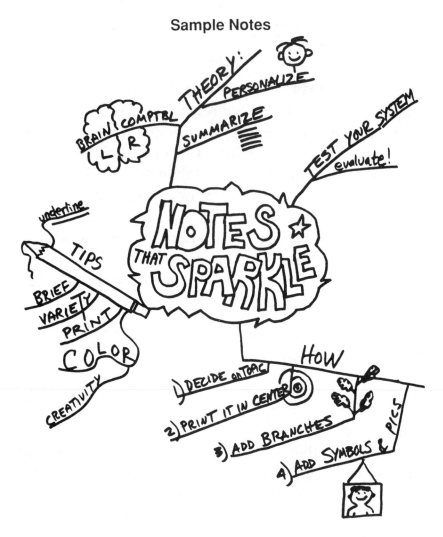

FIGURE 6-4

Recreate Your Notes

The last step in notetaking is the most important one. Once you have completed your notes for class, test yourself. Either your notes worked for you or they didn't. The way you test yourself is simple: On a blank piece of paper, recreate your notes from memory. If you're able to recreate 80 to 90 percent or better, congratulations. If it's anything less than that, you need to make some changes in the way you take notes. That means you must create a more useful format, maybe something that meets your own personal learning style better. Here are some of the variables that you can change:

Sample Notes for Chemistry

These notes, based on the format for exact sciences, include subject description, laws, examples, problems to solve, and solutions. Here is a sample:

Notes, p. 114

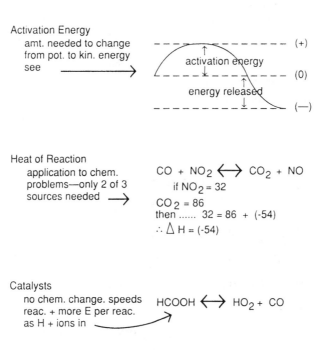

Activation Energy
  amt. needed to change
  from pot. to kin. energy
  see ⟶

activation energy (+) (0)
energy released (—)

Heat of Reaction
  application to chem.
  problems—only 2 of 3
  sources needed ⟶

$CO + NO_2 \longleftrightarrow CO_2 + NO$
  if $NO_2 = 32$
$CO_2 = 86$
then ...... $32 = 86 + (-54)$
$\therefore \Delta H = (-54)$

Catalysts
  no chem. change. speeds
  reac. + more E per reac.
  as H + ions in

$HCOOH \longleftrightarrow HO_2 + CO$

FIGURE 6-5

Sample Notes for Law Texts

This format helps to organize a law case quickly and clearly. While a third-year law student would look for a different approach from that of a first-year student, the basic information is the same.

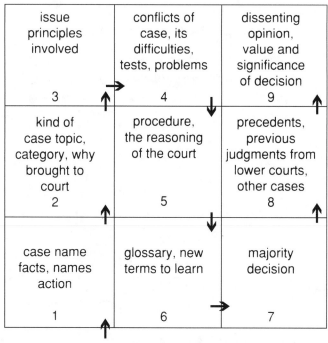

FIGURE 6-6

– Use more pictures and illustrations.

– Print instead of writing in script.

– Color code your key ideas—one color per idea.

– Organize the material differently.

– Use less detail.

– Use more diversity of print size and caps.

There's only one reason you're taking notes—for

Sample Notes for Novels: Type A

This format includes background on author, characters, settings, problems, events, crises, and solutions.

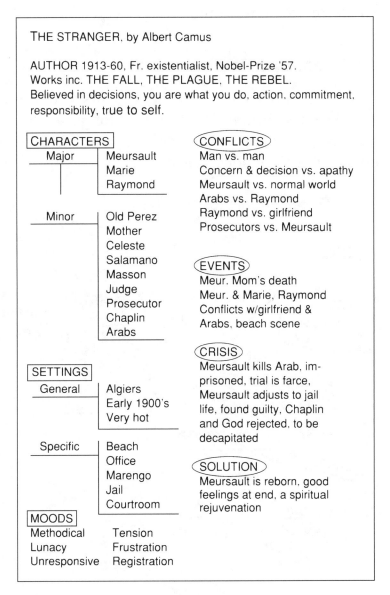

THE STRANGER, by Albert Camus

AUTHOR 1913-60, Fr. existentialist, Nobel-Prize '57.
Works inc. THE FALL, THE PLAGUE, THE REBEL.
Believed in decisions, you are what you do, action, commitment,
responsibility, true to self.

CHARACTERS
Major	Meursault
	Marie
	Raymond
Minor	Old Perez
	Mother
	Celeste
	Salamano
	Masson
	Judge
	Prosecutor
	Chaplin
	Arabs

SETTINGS
General	Algiers
	Early 1900's
	Very hot
Specific	Beach
	Office
	Marengo
	Jail
	Courtroom

MOODS
Methodical	Tension
Lunacy	Frustration
Unresponsive	Registration

CONFLICTS
Man vs. man
Concern & decision vs. apathy
Meursault vs. normal world
Arabs vs. Raymond
Raymond vs. girlfriend
Prosecutors vs. Meursault

EVENTS
Meur. Mom's death
Meur. & Marie, Raymond
Conflicts w/girlfriend &
Arabs, beach scene

CRISIS
Meursault kills Arab, im-
prisoned, trial is farce,
Meursault adjusts to jail
life, found guilty, Chaplin
and God rejected, to be
decapitated

SOLUTION
Meursault is reborn, good
feelings at end, a spiritual
rejuvenation

FIGURE 6-7

learning. If you're learning, great; you'll do well on any test or class questions. If not, change what you're doing. Notetaking can be a lot of fun *if* it's done creatively, *if* you test its effectiveness before the test, and *when* it pays off for you at test time.

Experiment and Apply

It's a common occurrence for students to develop a notetaking system and stick with it for years. They'll often change classes, change teachers, or even change schools. If their grades are average or below, they'll

Sample Notes for Novels: Type B

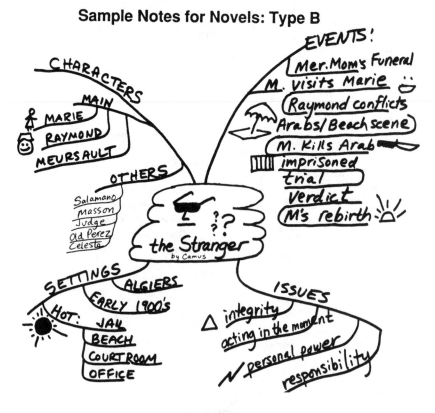

FIGURE 6-8

Sample Notes for History

Categorize your information so that you will follow the flow of events better. This format allows a better understanding of details as well as major events.

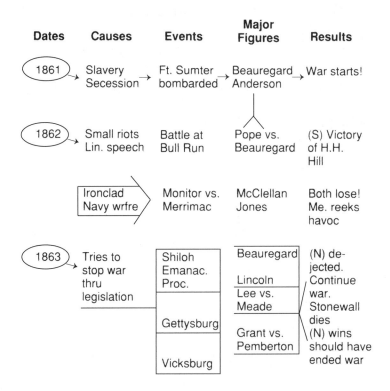

THE CIVIL WAR

Dates	Causes	Events	Major Figures	Results
1861	Slavery Secession	Ft. Sumter bombarded	Beauregard Anderson	War starts!
1862	Small riots Lin. speech	Battle at Bull Run	Pope vs. Beauregard	(S) Victory of H.H. Hill
	Ironclad Navy wrfre	Monitor vs. Merrimac	McClellan Jones	Both lose! Me. reeks havoc
1863	Tries to stop war thru legislation	Shiloh Emanac. Proc.	Beauregard Lincoln Lee vs. Meade	(N) dejected. Continue war. Stonewall dies
		Gettysburg Vicksburg	Grant vs. Pemberton	(N) wins should have ended war

FIGURE 6-9

often still keep their current system of notetaking, never suspecting that it may be a significant contributing factor to their grades. But *how* you take notes can make the difference between whether you understand the material or not, whether you make meaning out of it or not, or whether you recall it or not. If your system, whatever it is, fails you, it's time to switch. Here are some of the variables you can change to make them work better:

– Make the content more relevant to you.

– Increase the quantity and quality of pictures, symbols, and illustrations.

Sample Notes for Philosophy

In these notes, the left-hand side was prepared in advance, from the texts. Then the page of notes is taken to the class lecture so that traditional comments can be made on the right-hand side.

Aristotle's Critique of Spartan Constitution

BACKGROUND ON ARTIST
    Current society is ?
    Scien-philos-astron-
    "A is A," concretes,
    the realistic, specifics
 	
A's ANALYSIS OF S.C.
    (–) pop. mngmnt.
    (–) laws
        property laws
    bribes $
    no election of ovrsrs
    (-) treasury low on $
    (+) excess lifetime offcrs
    (+) must add soldiers
 	
(Q's FOR CLASS)
    implications of his crit.
    justified?
    Compr/contr w/US
        Constit.
    define "polis"
        "Ephoralty"	

FIGURE 6-10

Sample Text Notes

These notes show the use of a variety of techniques useful in taking brief, well-organized notes from a textbook.

THE WORLDLY PHILOSOPHER
by Robert Heibroner
Chapter 3—"The Wonderful World of Adam Smith"

BACKGROUND ON ENGLAND

Social Scene
Theology
Morality
Coal Mines

PERS. BIOG.

born 1723
Scotland
good student
U. of Glasgow
trav. Europe
died 1790

PERSONALITY TRAITS

friendly
nervous habits
well-known
absent-minded

MAJOR INFLUENCES ON HIM

Chas. Townshend (Ger.)
Dr. Quesnay (Fr.)
Ben Franklin (U.S.)

PUBLISHED WORKS

1759—Theory of Moral Sentiments
1776—Wealth of Nations
a revolutionary book
all encompassing

PHILOSOPHY

General

"Laws of Market"
Self-Interest is imp.
favors competition
specialization
whatever was
cheaper, simpler,
rational, expedient,
unregulated

Law of Accumulation

favors accum.
if re-channeled
into society

Law of Population

as productivity
increases/decreases
population
varies
proportionately

FIGURE 6-11

- Boost contrasts in color and size of print.
- Make notes more personalized and less generic.
- Make lettering in upper and lower case, not all caps.
- Make the lettering in print, not script style.
- Note which particular colors are used; intense is better.
- Location. Note where on your notes you recall or forget information.
- Experiment with more and less simple versus detailed information.
- Make the words more connected versus free-floating data.
- Experiment with the size of the mind map.
- Vary the use of thin and thick lettering.
- Make your notes tell a story as opposed to being disconnected.
- Have your notes relate to existing information as opposed to something new.
- Design the notes to evoke strong emotions.
- Create the notes while the material is at eye level or higher for best recall.

Experiment with these suggestions until you find the style that works well every time. You've got to get scientific about something as important as your learning and schoolwork. If your notes aren't working, change them. The list above will be at least one form of a checklist for you. Have fun and try several styles. One of them is sure to work for you!

Lecture Notetaking Responsibilities

Responsibility	Objective	Procedure
Listen	Anticipate your purpose.	Decide if you need to remember everything in the lecture or only main ideas. Determine what material you will be responsible for on a test. Determine if the lecture is a complement to your reading assignment or new material.
	Spend most of your time listening, not taking notes.	Listen to understand. Listen for entire ideas. Summarize ideas. Determine the main points. Decide how the main points are being made.
	Think and concentrate as you listen.	Note examples given. Decide if you agree with the main points. Determine if your previous knowledge allows you to interpret the information differently from the presentation. Try to recall the lecture so that you could present the information covered to someone else.
Take Notes	Be brief.	Write main ideas first. Write details if time allows.
	Use key words.	Write down key words that will allow recall of additional information presented.
	Use symbols.	Take notes using symbols, underlining pictures, cartoons, and arrows.
	Have extra supplies.	Carry spare pens, pencils, and paper.
	Review and reorganize.	Go over notes, rewrite or add extra information while they are fresh in your mind.

FIGURE 6-12

Review These Points

Learn Notetaking Skills
Summarize, Don't Duplicate
Create Your Own Style
Vary Your Print Size
Learn Subject Formats
Use Creative Approaches
Keep Notes Together
Recreate Your Notes
Experiment and Apply

7

MATH AND SCIENCE:
Strategies for Success

Each subject has its quirks and angles for optimal learning. That's why, if you have five or six classes, you'll get higher grades in one class than another. Certainly your interest level, the teacher, and the time of the day affect your learning. But if you're an active, hands-on learner, you may have a tough time with highly abstract subjects, no matter when they're taught and who's teaching them. If you had a template or list of strategies for success in each subject, it would be much easier. We will do just that for math, since it is an example of a subject that has those quirks and angles. As an example, the following is a list of what is a bit different about math for success (you'll find that some of these apply to sciences, too).

MATH STRATEGIES

- **It's rarely taught cooperatively**—with partners, groups, or teams. But to understand it and succeed at it, math often requires a lot of discussion and feedback.

- **It is rarely taught concretely,** so you don't get to use your hands to build models, to hold things, to find and touch angles and problems. But to succeed at math often requires a strong representation of what you're doing, and it's tough to do it all in your mind.

– **It is rarely taught with real world relevance.** While this is changing, most of the theorems, axioms, formulas, and problems seem quite distant from your everyday life. But making things relevant is one of the best ways to learn.

– **It is rarely taught globally,** with the big picture in mind. It is usually taught in small, microchunks and in pieces so small that it's hard to find out where you're going and what belongs to what and where it all fits in. The best way to learn math is to start with the big picture and work down to the smallest piece.

Having said all these things about math, the good news is that it is slowly changing. More and more schools are using strategies that make it easier and easier to learn. But until your school adopts some of these more learner-friendly approaches to teaching it, here are some things you can do.

Keep Up with Daily Assignments

There are some subjects in which you can fall behind a bit and still catch up. That happens to almost everyone. No problem, right? Well, in math, it can be deadly. Nearly every principle and example is built upon the previous one. It is one of those subjects you can't cram for. It's like learning to play a musical instrument; you cannot move on to play a harder piece until you have mastered an easier one. It is better for you to do two problems or to study for five minutes each day, than to do twenty problems each weekend. If you recognize that you are getting behind, stop the presses! Call an emergency! Get help ASAP!

Get Coaching Early

We just mentioned what you have to do to keep up or get ahead. But there's more. Find a mentor (it could be almost anyone who knows math) for the length of the course. You might get a tutor. Or, you might see your teacher. Get a teacher's aide or another student to help you. Remember, even the best pros (golfers, quarterbacks, track stars, basketball players, and so on) have coaches.

Get a Study Buddy

This person has to be one who knows the subject much better than you. The ideal is to make a "study trade." Is there something you know well, some help you could trade in exchange for the help you're getting? If not, get a study buddy anyway. Use your study buddy every week, not just when you are having a tough time. If you don't understand something, ask the teacher (or your mentor) *that day*!

Learn the Vocabulary

Know every key word inside and out. Test yourself! If your memory is less than 100 percent, go to work. Use memory associations. Use symbols. Use colored pens and pictures. Make cartoons out of the words. Put them on flashcards. Study those words, and study them with specific examples.

The Power of Mental Models

Most math teachers have a way of approaching math problems that is so confident, so flippant, so automatic. But they weren't born that way. Somehow, over time, they developed a way of thinking mathematically. Their mental model provides them with the basic framework for how they approach all math problems. It might consist of them first putting on an imaginary math hat. That's the thinking cap that says to them, "All problems can be solved; some are just easier than others." Then they know the magic sequence of steps to take when trying to solve a problem. They know what to try first and what to do next, and they know what to do if plan A fails. It's the accumulated years of math wisdom. This mental model may be like the key to the vault at Fort Knox to you. It might look something like the diagram that follows, but you'll want to find out exactly what it is for the class you're in.

Master the Formulas

There are many ways to memorize formulas: Put them on 3" × 5" flashcards, color them in, and carry them around, constantly testing yourself. Or, draw them out, color them, and put them up on a big poster you then hang on the wall. Or, learn them to music. Put on your special study tape and read a key formula; pause, then reread and pause again, letting the music fill in the pauses.

SAMPLE MENTAL MODEL FOR MATHEMATICS

Start With Success
Mindset

↓

Determine Problem

↓

Set Goals

↓

Establish Rules
and Procedures

↓

Begin Problem-Solving

↓   ↓

SUCCESS   SETBACK

Recheck Figures
Redefine Problem
Reread Problem

↓

SUCCESS

↓

GET HELP:

Study Buddy

Books-Computer

Teacher Aide

↓

SUCCESS
OR
REGROUP

FIGURE 7-1

Take Super-Accurate Notes

In math, notes have to be exact because the slightest mistake completely changes the meaning of a problem. Your notes should include the following:

1. main idea or key theorem
2. definitions
3. examples
4. rules, guidelines, tips
5. all diagrams, sample problems
6. teacher remarks that help make things clear

Divide your notetaking page into two columns. Keep words in the right column and examples in the left column. Spread out your information—paper is cheap! This leaves room to go back and add things later to boost comprehension.

Find the Pattern

Many times, a list or page of math problems is actually *one problem* presented 20 different ways. What is the pattern? Ask for help. Figure out what one thing happens in each of those problems. Once you find it, you'll be able to answer many more problems successfully. Work on the problems in your book with answers in the back, and talk your way through each one. When finished, you must know both the answer *and the procedure*. Talking to yourself keeps your attention and awareness high, plus it locks the learning into your memory.

INCANDESCENT

Give Meaning to Theorems

Make the numbers mean something. Make up stories. Use crazy-sounding names so that you'll remember them forever. For example, $E = MC^2$ becomes "Eric (that's my name) equals M.C. Hammer played twice."

Pretest Yourself

Test yourself on a dozen problems without using your textbook or help of any kind. Make it a timed test. Find out what you know and don't know. Improve yourself! Make up test questions twice a week so you can think the way the teacher thinks at test time.

When you feel you are done with your homework, review several problems. Explain them out loud or to a study buddy. Your explanation is your review.

Ask Yourself Some Questions

First, read the problem, reread the problem, gather information, analyze the type of problem, and sort out vocabulary or symbols. Next, ask yourself a series of questions. The answers will usually steer you in the right direction:

- What is this problem really asking for?
- How can I restate the problem?
- Could I use a diagram or picture to help out?
- Where is the backup information I need?
- Can I make an estimate?
- How will I compute this problem?

– Is there someone I can go to for help?

– Is my answer within reasonable boundaries?

– Can I prove it?

– Do I know both the procedure and the solution?

– Could I duplicate my success again and again?

Change Texts

If your book is hard to understand, get another that you can understand better. Keep your old one, but get one by another author, one that is used in another class, or one from the library. Feel free to go down in difficulty. It's no shame; the biggest shame would be for you to fail a course that you could have passed.

SCIENCE STRATEGIES

In the past, it was assumed that it was only the nerds who did well in science. Those days are gone. Science is not for nerds; it's for everyone. It combines a unique mix of linear, sequential thinking with random creative thinking. It's a wonderful subject because it's as real-world as you can get. The products you buy, the foods you eat, the cars you ride in are all products of science. There are many strategies to learning science that you can use. Pick the ones that you're not doing now and find out what works best.

Sample Notes

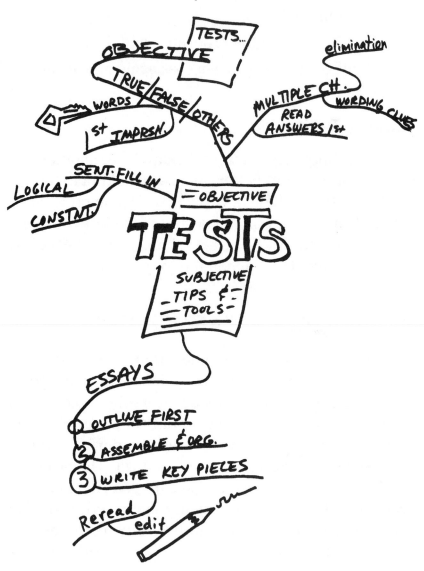

FIGURE 7-2

Take a Personal Field Trip

Is there a place that could better explain some theory or chapter in the textbook? How about a local science museum or exploratorium? Ask the teacher for other ways to learn about the topic.

Know Where You Stand

Stay in touch with your learning. Make sure you know your terms, assignments, and scores. Do what it takes to stay even or get ahead. Find a tutor. See your teacher. Get a teacher's aide or other student. There's nothing embarrassing about getting help. It's a lot better than getting a D or an F.

Find a Science Video, TV Show, or CD

There are many new shows on public television or the Discovery Channel that feature science. Some video stores even rent science videos. The media center at your school may have some videos or good material on CDs. Some of them are fun; others are more serious. They can be a great way to learn or reinforce existing learning. Get a TV program listing and look ahead each week to find out if there's a show about something you're learning. Also, you'll be able to get help on the Internet. You may find out how many others have already solved the problem you're facing.

Try Things Out at Home

You'd be surprised how many concepts have a simple do-at-home angle to them. Ask your teacher if there's something you could try out at home. This will not only let you work at your own pace, but you'll bring much more relevance to it. Many household or garage experiments require no money to make; they use simple items found around the home. You can perform physics experiments with a balloon, a soft drink bottle, an aerosol can, and piece of paper. Which ones? Ask your teacher!

Talk to Friends

There are sometimes several teachers at your school who teach the same basic classes. Do you have a friend in another science class? If so, ask him or her what they're doing and learning. You'd be surprised; sometimes another teacher will make a concept so simple just by presenting it differently. Ask, ask, ask.

Pay Attention in Labs

Many science teachers let the class perform experiments. Some classes have a science lab. Many students use the lab as a chance to relax and visit with their friends. Use the experiment or lab as a source of learning. Today, teachers are using the labs more and more as part of the formal grading process. Ask, ask, and ask some more, until you understand exactly what is happening.

Review These Points

Math Strategies
Keep Up with Daily Assignments
Get Coaching Early
Get a Study Buddy
Learn the Vocabulary
The Power of Mental Models
Master the Formulas
Take Super-Accurate Notes
Find the Pattern
Give Meaning to Theorems
Pretest Yourself
Ask Yourself Some Questions
Change Texts

Science Strategies
Take a Personal Field Trip
Know Where You Stand
Find a Science Video, TV Show, or CD
Try Things Out at Home
Talk to Friends
Pay Attention in Labs

8

MEMORY MADE EASY:
You Can Recall More!

We all wish, at times, that we could remember more than we do. But it's good to forget some things—daily trivia as well as unpleasant experiences. To your brain, anything related to a strong emotion or survival (food and safety, for example) is very important. Those things you'll recall with little effort. But you need to learn how to remember what *you* think are the important things. And that's a bit tricky. Memory is a process, not a single spot in the brain. There is no single memory center. So when we say someone has a good memory, what we really mean is that the person is good at the process of selective retrieval. The activity or skill of remembering can be improved in the same way that the skill at chess or tennis can. This is good news—you are not stuck with a poor memory. But to be able to use it more effectively, it helps if you understand it.

HOW DOES YOUR MEMORY WORK?

Only recently have scientists unlocked the mysteries of how our brain's amazing memory system works. You have many ways to remember things. Good notes are your best, natural, easiest way to learn, store, and recall things exactly when and how you need them.

Memory scientists say you have three ways to remember things; you can use your **mind** for the words, use your **body** to trigger the memory, and use **space** (different locations and circumstances) to trigger the learning.

Use Your Mind

When you use your mind, you memorize important elements with repetition, with memory links, association, review, key words, and memory tricks. All of these can work, but they do require strong motivation on your part. This is the type of memory you try to use for words, names, places, dates, definitions, facts, and a million other things required by school.

As an example:

The names of the five Great Lakes are H-O-M-E-S (Huron, Ontario, Michigan, Erie, and Superior). The horizontal lines on a musical staff are E-G-B-D-F (Every Good Boy Does Fine). The colors of the rainbow are Roy G. Biv (red, orange, yellow, green, blue, indigo, and violet).

Use Your Body

You can remember something by acting it out, doing it, building something, feeling it, smelling it, tasting it, teaching it to a friend, hearing it, or drawing it.

As an example:

You remember things you did in a lab (chemistry, biology, or physics). You remember things you did in a language class (skits or role play).

Also, your body remembers things by how you felt when you learned it. If you take a test while stressed out, you'll forget too much. Whatever the test will be like, study that way. If you feel stressed, practice your studying (after you've learned it) by reviewing things fast, under time pressure. That way, your body and brain are more used to the testing conditions and you'll do better at test time.

Use Space

We remember what we learned by *where* we learned it and the *circumstances* of the learning. Study one subject at school, one in your bedroom, one in the living room, another in the library, etc. These help your brain link up a place in space with the content. But there's more: Use different colored pens for each chapter you study. Make different-shaped notes and test yourself by recalling your own notes from memory or redoing them for practice.

As an example:

> If you study in the same room in which you'll be taking your final exam, studies show your recall will be higher. If you have five chapters to study, study each one in a different place so you'll have separate distinct memories of each.

Which of the three types of memory is best for you? Figure out what you have been using that has worked well for you. Has it been notes, movement, or locations? Are you better at mind, body, or space learning? Whatever you do best, start doing more of that today.

Review one of the three ideas in one corner of the room. Move to another corner and review the next one. With each idea, pretend you're eating a different food (smell it and taste it). Then do the last one in another part of the room (this uses both body and space memory!). It sounds wild, but it works!

FOCUS ATTENTION

Being aware is the first step to developing better recall. Begin to notice the part of the page on which information is located. Notice how it's presented and take an extra look at visual aids. Surprisingly, many people do not even know such basic things as what color their walls and curtains are, what their license plate number is, or even their social security number. Knowing these things may not be very important, but learning to be more aware of your surroundings can be very helpful in developing memory skills.

How to improve attention: Practice on the little things. Pay attention to new sounds and old sounds. Pay attention to signs, who is ahead of you or behind you. Act as if you're a detective or spy and pretend everything is important. Simply practice being attentive.

GET IT RIGHT

Make sure that you correctly understand the data. This sounds like a simple rule, but, particularly in the case of remembering statistics, people rarely focus on the numbers themselves; they pay attention to the significance of them. At gatherings where new people are introduced, you're particularly focused on who is there, how important the gathering is, or the noise level. We often want to be polite or even feel smart, so we rarely ask a second time for the person's name. The same thing happens in a class at school. A teacher says something, but when we don't understand it, we often let it go and hope we'll figure it out later (which we often do). Sometimes it is lost forever, though. Get in the habit of getting it right the first time.

How to improve this habit: Start the very next chance you get. Either from television or in person, make sure you get a name right, or a new address right, or a new vocabulary word right. Then repeat it for clarification and reinforcement. Double check with someone else or with the source to confirm your memory.

TELL YOURSELF YOU CAN

Although the topic is still controversial, there are still many researchers who claim that the struggle to recall is a performance problem, not an imprinting or storage problem. They say we simply need the correct triggers for the particular memory and it comes forth, and that it's more a matter of just three things for retrieval:

1. review and rehearsal
2. associations in the same context in which we learned it
3. learning to match similar physiological states

That's why affirmations and positive reinforcement are not simply pop psychology. It is a fact that you can recall nearly everything. Unfortunately, the circumstances and associations are rarely available for everything—but telling yourself you *can* remember is part of developing a healthy self-image.

Faith in yourself relaxes and encourages stronger mental processes by opening previously closed thought channels. We can usually do only what we believe we can. Most of the time, the incentive to remember information is already there, but every object of memory is made much stronger when you intensify your desire to recall. If you met someone at a party who interested you, your desire to remember his or her name and phone number would be strong. Similarly, when you know you'll be tested on a book, your efforts increase appreciably.

How to improve this habit: Start with a new attitude about memory and recall. Avoid saying, "Oops, I gotta go back. I realize I forgot something." The more accurate way is to say, "Hey, I just remembered something; I gotta go back." In other words, you *never* forget anything—you just *remembered it later* than you wanted to!

UNDERSTAND IT WELL

Though it may sound obvious, make sure you thoroughly understand what you want to remember. This rule applies equally to poetry, mathematics, history, sciences, and related fields. If something makes sense, it's much easier to recall. We learned in an earlier chapter the value of making it meaningful. That may be a critical ingredient to developing a greater understanding.

How to boost understanding: Use multiple pathways for learning. If you learn the material initially from a lecture, then draw it or make pictures. Watch a video or a movie. Stop in on a discussion group. As long as you switch the way you learn it, your chances increase for new understanding and meaning.

BE CREATIVE

One of the most powerful ways to recall is to unleash your imagination. It seems that our brain is better designed to recall what is unusual than what is normal. Whenever you can take your more common stream of notes and turn them into something off the wall and creative, it's going to stand out more and you're going to recall it better later on.

How to use this idea: Turn your text material into pictures, change names into pictures, exaggerate, and be artistic by putting some color into the data, associating it with sight, sound, taste, and smell. Or, you may want to turn key phrases into a rhyme. For some reason, our brain seems to recall rhymes far better than simple nonrhyming material.

MAKE STRONG MENTAL PICTURES

Often called the key to memorizing, mental pictures enable your mind to work in its more natural state.

Usually, your mind stores images and pictures, not words. When you think of milk, do you picture the four letters m-i-l-k? Most people picture a glass or carton of milk. Using the normal storage system, by creating mental pictures, you can remember data much more easily. Change words and ideas into pictures and simply study the pictures, not the words. There are several books that are helpful, such as *Creative Visualization* by Shakti Gawain. *The Great Memory Book*, by Karen Markowitz and Eric Jensen, is a very readable and practical resource as well.

Here's another way to improve your memory with pictures. Did you know that you can use your brain like a TV set to build your recall of any item? You can.

You simply need to think of the item, then enhance it the same way you would enhance a video in the production studio. Make the colors stronger, sharpen the focus, make the image bigger and brighter, add a favorite confidence-building sound track, and put in your favorite feelings. As you add those components, you'll discover that you suddenly have a better memory of that item.

How to Practice Mental Pictures

Link one word to another in order to form associations. Your memory skills will improve if you practice creating mental pictures about what you want to recall. The more unusual and absurd the mental picture you create, the more likely it is that you will be able to recall the word or information associated with it. Use these four ideas to create vivid mental pictures:

1. Imagine some kind of *action* taking place.
2. Form an image that is *out of proportion*.
3. Create in your mind an *exaggerated version* of the subject.
4. Substitute and *reverse* a normal role.

For example, in order to remember to mail a letter, imagine the letter carrying you out to the mailbox and stuffing you inside. Improve your memory skills by practicing word associations using mental pictures. For example, in associating the words *table* and *dance*, first form a clear picture of a table in your mind. Visualize a table that you use frequently, one that is familiar to you. In order to associate *table* with *dance*, imagine the table standing up on two legs, dancing wildly, with the other two legs spinning in the air.

Because it is such an absurd picture, it will stick in your mind. Each time you think of table, you will think of dance. The linking of words can continue in a similar manner. If you wish to next link the word *dance* to *duck*, for example, you might create a mental picture of a huge, six-foot-tall, all white, overfed, potbellied duck dancing and whirling, with feathers flying. By using the method of linking through mental pictures, you have created a chain of associations: *table* to *dance, dance* to *duck*. In this way, you never try to memorize more than one word at a time. The process is all done with mental pictures. The system of forming associations by using the link method will help you to memorize lists of names, places, events, items, or almost anything. Figure 8-1 includes additional ideas on how to use association.

USE THE POWER OF ASSOCIATION

Probably the simplest method of remembering is by association, the process of recalling one item because another reminded you of it. This system requires no more than some awareness and a quick mental picture. Some researchers say that all of our recall is simply

Forming Associations Between Random Words

Item.............Think of...................................Then associate......

table	an enormous table, or a particular table, such as your kitchen table	
dance	imagine a dance	imagine the table dancing, up on two legs
duck	an enormous, overstuffed, six-foot-tall duck, white with orange feet and bill	imagine the duck doing this wild dance
walnuts	millions of walnuts falling out of the sky	imagine the walnuts between the toes
toes	your own toes	imagine huge walnuts between your toes
mirror	very small mirrors the size of a stamp	picture mirrors on the toes instead of toenails
bear	picture a huge brown bear, with your clothes on	imagine the bear seeing himself in the mirror
canoe	picture a dugout canoe	picture the bear paddling around in a canoe
necklace	an enormous, long one	imagine the necklace draped around the canoe
fire	crackling and extra hot	imagine the necklace so hot it's on fire— remove it!

FIGURE 8-1

association. The trick is to learn how to evoke the appropriate associations at the right time.

How to use this idea: If you wanted to remember to bring a pen to class, Post-its can work. Or, simply imagine black, gooey ink all over the doorknob where you live. Make a quick but strong mental picture of it. Then, when you leave for class, reaching for the door-knob will trigger the mental picture of ink, and you'll remember your pen.

PRACTICE RECALLING UNDER MANY CONDITIONS

An interesting finding about memory revealed that we have our best memory when we match the learning and the recall mind-body states. In other words, if you're relaxed and casual while you study and relaxed and casual while you take an exam, you'll do better than if there's a mismatch. If you practice recalling only under prime conditions, information may elude you dur-ing test time.

How to use this idea:: When you have critical infor-mation to remember, create flash cards on 3" × 5" index cards to take with you. Then whenever you have a break—at mealtime, while relaxing, or in the library—study the cards and practice recalling.

This strategy bears repeating. Ask yourself, "How do I usually respond to tests?" If you usually get tense and stressed, then you'll want to make sure you study and learn to recall under those very same conditions. That will "prime" your brain to be able to better recall when you need it. Give yourself study deadlines, have a watch or clock handy, and give yourself rigorous time goals to teach your brain how to respond under pressure. You'll be pleasantly surprised at how much you'll be able to recall later.

REDUCE INTERFERENCE

Apparently our mind needs down time to sort and categorize information for long-term storage and retrieval. There are many sources of distractions that can hamper this process, including strong emotions, competing subjects, and diet. Research quoted by *Mastering the Information Age* author Michael McCarthy indicates that the ideal is a restful time directly before and directly after learning new material. Your mind will then have time to relax, sort, and store the necessary information. Scientists have discovered that our brain uses the relaxed sleep time to do some mental housecleaning. We actually forget many things on purpose. That's a normal part of our brain's nighttime operations, to get rid of memories that we think are unnecessary. This also works with the BEM concept for better recall. We remember material best from the beginning (B), second best from the end (E), and our recall is weakest on material from the middle (M).

How to use this idea: Invest more time on the middle to allow for the BEM tendency. Avoid studying two similar subjects (like two science or literature classes) back to back. When you're finished studying, take a short nap or go to sleep for the night.

LEARN WHOLES, NOT JUST PARTS

Whether the subject is a Shakespearean play or an assignment in anatomy, our mind recalls best with context, a global understanding, and complete pictures to remember. Even if you have to memorize only one part of a chapter, become familiar with all of it. We find our way around a shopping mall better when we find the directory that shows us where everything is and tells us, "You are here!"

How to use this idea: To learn about a part of the human body, learn something first about all of it. To learn about lines and angles, get an overview of geometry first. If you have to learn why a local beach has low and high tides, it would be much easier if you also discussed how our tides are simply opposite those on the other side of the world. The big picture provides a better answer than a local example. One of the best ways to get an overview is to watch a TV program, video, or movie on the entire topic.

REPETITION: USE THE MATERIAL

In spite of all we know about memory, very few things have replaced repetition. Why? Every time you have a thought or engage in an activity, the neural pathways are strengthened; over time, they become a habit. With enough usage, they become nearly indelible. As a child, you heard and used your own name so often, that it became indelibly imprinted. While this tool is not the only tool for remembering things, it still works.

We use both a long-term and a short-term memory and most of what we take in goes into our short-term memory. For example, when you look up a number in the phone book, you remember it just long enough to dial it. Then you promptly forget it. That is, of course, short-term. To get data transferred to our long-term recall system, we need to engage our learning and use it for reinforcement. The ideal way to study and memorize is to reinforce your learning sufficiently so that it is put into your long-term memory.

Frequently review, repeat, recite, and use the material you wish to remember. Almost any information learned becomes familiar, and even second nature, through usage. Try to integrate the data into daily usage.

How to use this idea: Right after a learning activity—within ten minutes, and again within 48 hours—refresh your memory through a review. Spend six one-hour sessions on a subject, rather than six straight hours. Make up flashcards and carry them around, reviewing when you have a spare moment.

1. Make up flashcards from 3" × 5" cards.

2. Take your most important ideas and make colorful, interesting graphic reminders of them in the form of posters.

3. Make up a simple audiotape (or CD) of the key ideas and listen to it. Make the key concepts rhyme.

4. Talk to people about what you learn. Sound corny? Not if it's all part of a study group where people would talk about things like that anyway.

Remember that there are many ways to remember and recall key things for school. Using repetition is just one (and not always the most fun or effective) of the strategies for better recall. While it's true that it does work, using multiple strategies is the most effective. It gives your brain more pathways to use when you need to recall that information later.

Review These Points

How Does Your Memory Work?
Use Your Mind
Use Your Body
Use Space

Focus Attention

Get It Right

Tell Yourself You Can

Understand It Well

Be Creative

Make Strong Mental Pictures
How to Practice Mental Pictures

Use The Power of Association

Practice Recalling Under Many Conditions

Reduce Interference

Learn Wholes, Not Just Parts

Repetition: Use the Material

WORD POWER:
Vocabulary and Spelling

If you think a good vocabulary would help you get straight A's, you are right. In nearly every field, the successful person also has a powerful vocabulary. Scholars believe a good vocabulary is so important that it is a major part of most intelligence tests. Students with an effective vocabulary excel not only in English, but also in math, science, and business. And the reason they excel is not because they are any smarter, but because they can better express themselves. In almost any business in the country, the higher an employee's position, the better his or her working vocabulary. Yet, how can you improve your vocabulary?

EXPAND YOUR READING

If you do what you've always been doing, then you'll get what you've always gotten. Read what you've always been reading and your vocabulary will be the same, too. The secret? Expand your reading territory. Many periodicals are written for people with a sixth-grade education. In order to improve your vocabulary, read newspapers and magazines of high journalistic quality. Some excellent publications are *Harpers*, *The Nation*, *Atlantic Monthly*, *New Republic*, *National Review*, *Commentary*, *Scientific American*, *Psychology Today*,

Discover, and *The New Yorker*. Reading material of this caliber will help you learn many new words. Should you subscribe to all these publications? Of course not! Simply read them on-line or go to the library.

TRY OUT NEW WORDS

Use the dictionary to learn new or unfamiliar words. Jot down definitions on a notepad that you keep posted. Refer to it often to refresh your memory. Use new words as often as possible, even to the point of overuse. Make it a goal to learn a new word each week. You will be amazed at how quickly your vocabulary increases. Add new words to your daily vocabulary by consciously interjecting them into conversations until you feel comfortable using them.

BIRDS OF A FEATHER

Expressive, articulate speakers have a way of influencing others. Their ability to express themselves will encourage your use of new words. Your level of communication varies with the people with whom you converse. A college graduate has to simplify language in order to explain to a first grader how a president is elected. But the same person may use more difficult and specialized terminology when talking to a professor at school. Associating with people who have a good command of the English language will help to improve your vocabulary and your communication skills.

TAKE A LATIN OR GREEK CLASS

The English language evolved from many languages, but a large percentage of the words in our dictionary have a Latin or Greek origin. At a high school, college, or community adult education program, you can enroll in a class that will give you a good background in word origins and definitions. Here's the great part: Learning even some of the key Latin or Greek words will automatically give you the thousands of words that are related to those words. You may be surprised how much this helps. A biology major discovered that when it comes to studying the brain, the classic languages were like a "key to the vault." Here are some terms from the field of neuroscience and their roots in Greek or Latin. Their root words (on the right) give clues about their shape or function:

amygdala	almond
cortex	bark
cerebellum	little brain
glia	glue
hippocampus	seahorse

GET IN THE DICTIONARY AND THESAURUS HABIT

Whenever you come across a word that is unfamiliar to you, or that you don't understand, turn to the dictionary. It is the good speller who uses the dictionary. Get in the habit of referring to the dictionary, whether you are reading a newspaper or a scholarly

journal. The most important thing to remember when looking up definitions of new words is to not stop there. Make use of new words in your daily conversation every chance you get.

A thesaurus is another useful book for learning the meanings of words; it's simply a dictionary of synonyms. For each entry in a thesaurus, many words that have the same or similar meanings are listed. For example, *Roget's Thesaurus* lists 29 synonyms for the word *expert*, including master, medalist, genius, mastermind, prodigy, first fiddle, and connoisseur. A thesaurus is a lot of fun to use. Browse through one, and you may find words much more interesting.

UPGRADE YOUR SPELLING

Is spelling a dead art? No. In spite of computerized spell-checks, we still need to know how words are spelled when we write them. It is still a source of pride to be able to spell words correctly in front of others when speaking or showing something. It is still valuable to be able to get things right the first time. People form impressions about you in the first 30 seconds, and when you misspell key words, they may think you have less education or are simply sloppy in your work.

Start noticing how words are spelled when you read. Take a course in grammar or composition. Respond to class feedback; when your papers are returned to you, notice the spelling corrections. Sometimes it helps to have another person review your assignments. Pay attention to phonetic sounds, and listen carefully to how words are pronounced. A large percentage of the words in our language are spelled just the way they sound.

Three good ways to sharpen your spelling ability are to learn roots, suffixes, and prefixes. Root words build both spelling and comprehension skills. Figure 9-1 lists ten common roots. Learning them will instantly bring to your fingertips an understanding of hundreds of words. Some of the most commonly misspelled, misused words appear in Figure 9-2. Study the table to avoid confusing words that are spelled similarly or pronounced the same.

Common Word Roots

Root	Meaning	Usage
co/com/con	with, together	collaborate, combine, conjugal
bi	two, dual	bicycle, bipartisan, bicentennial
chron	time	chronology, chronicle, anachronism
gen	class, race, kind	gender, genre, genius, general
auto	self	automatic, autograph, autonomy, author
trans	across	transfer, transmit, transportation
gram/graph	write	epigram, telegram, graph, stenography
sub	under	submerge, submit, submarine
super, sur	above	supervise, superfluous, surpass, surtax
dic, dict	say	abdicate, diction, verdict
mal	bad	malevolent, dismal, malefactor
pro	before, forward, in favor of	proponent, propensity, proclivity
ab	from, away from	abduct, abstract, abnormal
dif/dis	not, apart	discord, disparity, differ
circum	around	circumnavigate, circumspect, circumference

FIGURE 9-1

Common Errors in Spelling and Usage

Word	Meaning	Usage
then	shows time	**Then** he went home.
than	compares	He is taller **than** I am.
weather	relating to climate	We had nice **weather** today.
whether	involves decision	I don't know **whether** it's right.
accept	to receive	Will he **accept** the gift?
except	to exclude	Everyone laughed **except** Bob.
lose	opposite of to find	I did not **lose** it.
loose	not tight	The belt was **loose**.
already	previously	It's **already** dinner time.
all ready	prepared	She was **all ready**.
its	shows possession	The dog wagged **its** tail.
it's	means it is	**It's** going to be hot.
they're	means they are	**They're** not at home.
there	usually shows location or opens a sentence	Sit over **there**.
their	shows possession	**Their** house.
like	do not use when you really mean "for example"	WRONG: My father is an awful driver. Like last week . . . RIGHT: My father is an awful driver. For example, last week . . .
altogether	entirely	It's **altogether** too soon.
all together	all in the same place	We're **all together** now.

FIGURE 9-2

Common Errors in Spelling and Usage
(continued)

Word	Meaning	Usage
break brake	to fracture, shatter, or ruin a stopping device	Don't **break** my heart. Set the parking **brake**.
adapt	to adjust, make suitable, remodel	As much as we may dislike the thought of it, we **adapt** to change quite easily.
adopt	to accept formally, take as one's own	After considerable discussion, the new bylaws were **adopted** by our association.
beside	at the side of	Walking **beside** his mother, he felt safe and content.
besides	in addition to, moreover	**Besides** an obsession for chocolates, I have a weakness for pecans as well.
stationary	fixed, standing still	The shadow of the tree remained **stationary** throughout the hot, breezeless afternoon.
stationery	writing supplies, writing paper	Hoping it would help his case, she had the letter typed on school **stationery**.
principal	most important	The **principal** purpose of the meeting was explained as soon as everyone had quieted down.
principle	basic belief or truth	Such **principles** of human nature as curiosity and greed do not show mankind.

FIGURE 9-2

Review These Points

Expand Your Reading
Try Out New Words
Birds of a Feather
Take a Latin or Greek Class
Get in the Dictionary and Thesaurus Habit
Upgrade Your Spelling

10

EVALUATING LITERATURE:
Be an Instant Critic

In school, you are often asked to evaluate short stories, poems, complete novels, or entire books. But the skills necessary for assessing a work of fiction may not be taught in some schools. The many levels of meaning of novels, plays, and poems can be understood by you. All it takes is a method of approach, and your desire to follow it through.

PREPARE FOR IT

Mindset is critical. Tell yourself that you *can* do it, you *can* do a good job of it, and you *can* get it done. Get together your fiction work and notepaper, and prepare to write. Before you start reading, look at the front and back covers, the preface, and foreword. Then browse through the book to learn the following:

1. How is the book structured? You'll want to learn the length of chapters, parts, or acts. Give your mind a mental sense of the shape of the work.

2. Who are the characters and where does the story take place? (Proper names and nouns will be easy to spot, so write them down.)

3. How is the title related to the story? You should have a few notes on the story before you begin reading.

4. Start making some guesses about the themes, the ideas, and the plots. It gets your mind going and it helps you to be ready for what's to come in the book.

MEET THE AUTHOR

There are some works where the author is less important (a dictionary, a manual of how to repair furniture, certain works of fiction, etc.). However, for the most part, nonfiction and fiction are an interpretation of some aspect of life as seen through the eyes of the author. Get to know that person and you'll gain insight into what he or she is writing about and why. Some of the best ways to meet an author are:

1. Ask your teacher for information on the author's life.

2. Read other books by the same author.

3. Check the book's jacket, introduction, preface, or publisher's notes.

4. Find a biography or autobiography of the author and learn as much as you can.

ORGANIZE THE INFORMATION

You know that some works of literature are easier than others. What makes them that way? Usually, it has to do with *organization* and *flow*. Comprehension and meaning come quickly when the story has unity and flows well. Discover the flow of ideas by organizing the information you have recorded into categories. Use the format illustrated in Figure 10-1 to organize your notes about characters, setting, moods, conflicts, events, complications, crises, and solutions. The list of characters should include a comment about each of the major ones and a listing of the minor ones.

Possible Format for Organizing Notes on Fiction

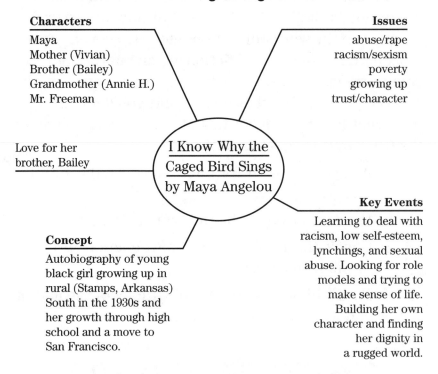

Characters
Maya
Mother (Vivian)
Brother (Bailey)
Grandmother (Annie H.)
Mr. Freeman

Issues
abuse/rape
racism/sexism
poverty
growing up
trust/character

Love for her
brother, Bailey

I Know Why the Caged Bird Sings by Maya Angelou

Concept
Autobiography of young black girl growing up in rural (Stamps, Arkansas) South in the 1930s and her growth through high school and a move to San Francisco.

Key Events
Learning to deal with racism, low self-esteem, lynchings, and sexual abuse. Looking for role models and trying to make sense of life. Building her own character and finding her dignity in a rugged world.

FIGURE 10-1

Usually there is one general setting, and many more specific ones, so list them in sequence. For moods, write down how the characters feel about their positions in the action of the story, as well as how you react to each character. Is it light fiction, a horror story, a mystery, or a satire? To analyze events, crises, and solutions, record happenings of importance in the plot, and the events that led to the crisis or turning point. Suddenly, the pressure is released, and momentum switches—a major decision is reached, the crisis is resolved, and the remainder of the story is usually a winding down.

Sometimes the author's solutions and viewpoints are presented in these last pages of the novel. By organizing your information around these elements of the plot, the different levels of meaning will surface quickly, and your understanding of the novel will increase.

PRIME THE MIND

What's so good about questions? Simple. They beg your mind to answer them. The more questions you ask, the more your mind has been primed for the answer. Your mind, then, will be more alert, subconsciously seeking the answers to each question. Ask questions early to get your mind into the story. Ask questions during the story to help understand it better. Ask questions after you finish to help you make meaning out of the story.

The questions that follow are designed to help you understand what the author is saying, how he or she says it, and why. They are fairly easy to answer if you review the list before you start your reading. Most students gather enough information to evaluate fiction; they just need a way to derive qualitative, meaningful data from it. Use the following questions to help you evaluate fiction:

- What is the subject area, the general idea(s)?
- Is there any personal inner motivation for the book's author?
- Was the book trying to entertain, persuade, etc.?
- Did the author successfully meet this goal?
- How did the book affect you?
- Could it have been more effective?
- What kinds of conflicts are presented? (Conflicts include man vs. man, man vs. nature, and man vs. himself.)
- Are they solved? How? How do you feel about the solution? Is it realistic?

When you think about asking questions, remember that there is not one single great question to ask. These are designed to help you uncover the heart and soul of the work. The process of asking, and the side thoughts you'll come up with, may end up being more valuable than the question itself. Some more questions follow. While you may not have to ask every single one (they may not even fit for the reading you're currently doing), the questions alone will get your brain going, so stick with it.

- Who was the main character in the novel?
- Does the main character represent the viewpoint of the author?

– What does the main character believe in?

– How do you feel about the main character? Why?

– How does the character try to meet his or her goals? Are these goals met?

– Toward which characters does the author seem to feel most sympathetic, and why?

– Do they represent a political, social, economic, or moral viewpoint? Which one?

The more questions you ask, the more answers you're likely to find. Let's keep asking a few more questions about the book:

– Are the characters convincing in their role? Were they believable, or supposed to be believable?

– What changes do the characters go through in the book?

– Did they change for the better or for the worse?

– What caused the change? What do the changes represent?

– On what does the author base the book—a historical solution or changing social trend? a recent disaster, politics, or inventions?

– How does this book fit into literature in general, or current historical perspective?

– What current social trends are dramatized?

– Was the story smooth or choppy?

– Did the book have impact? Would you recommend it to others?

SHARPEN YOUR QUESTIONS

The more you read, the better equipped you will be to analyze and critique fiction. If you want to critique Hemingway's *A Farewell to Arms*, there are several approaches you might choose. Read what others say about it and decide if you agree or disagree. You might decide to compare it with his other major works. For example, you might read *The Sun Also Rises* and contrast it to *A Farewell to Arms*. To be able to judge Hemingway's style, you might decide to study a variety of writing styles as typified by such American authors as Fitzgerald, Faulkner, Mailer, or Vonnegut.

Examine the author's objective.

- Is the author trying to inform, entertain, persuade or criticize? Did the author succeed?

- Was the dialogue meant to be realistic, and is it?

- What is the tone of the novel—sarcastic, hopeful, despairing? Is it effective?

- How long does the author spend on crucial sequences of events as compared with minor events?

- Analyze the characters. How are they introduced?

- Are any introduced and then forgotten? Why?

- Are the characters consistent in their behavior, or were they meant to be otherwise?

- Do the conversations fit each character's portrayal? Or do they contradict it?

These questions are the type that book critics keep in mind when they review a book. Does it sound like overkill? It is, a bit. But they do provide at least some kind of a structure for better understanding and critiquing the material. Here are a few more questions to bring into your thinking.

- Which character does the author favor and why?
- Determine the author's writing style and mechanics. Are any parts of the book so wordy that the plot suffers?
- Is all of the narration necessary?
- Is the sentence structure varied?
- How does the author balance main ideas with minor ones?
- Does the author keep you interested by creating a desire to continue reading?
- Do you react the way the characters do?
- Are you swept into the action?
- Does the book have a single unifying direction or theme?

All authors bring their childhood, adolescent, and adult life into their works, but with each author, it's a different degree of influence. Here are some ways to make sense of those. Ascertain the author's bias or viewpoint.

- What philosophies does the author seem to put forth?
- Does the book reflect the beliefs of Plato, Aristotle, existentialism, realism, or naturalism?
- Is it conservative, liberal, or a combination?

- At any point is the author illogical, very misin-formed, prejudiced, incomplete, incorrect, or inconsistent?
- How do the author's ideas fit into today's thinking?
- Is the story believable? Was it meant to be?
- Does the title fit the story?

As you can tell, there is practically an endless list of criteria by which you can judge an author and work. If you are cautious and thorough in your approach, you can evaluate and critique an author's work as well as anyone. And once you have explored these thoughts, you will not only have a critic's insight into fiction, but you will enjoy it much more. See Figure 10-2 for addi-tional guidelines.

DEVELOP A POINT OF VIEW

At this point, you'll have some strong ideas about what the author thinks and what shaped his or her thinking. Knowing these things can help you understand and appreciate the literary work. But there's more to think about.

- How do you feel about the author's values, opin-ions, and beliefs?
- Do you agree with them?
- Are the morals and ethics consistent with yours? In what ways?
- In what ways are they different?
- What would you say to the author?

– In what ways have times changed since the book was written that might alter the perceptions of the reader?

Can you make your point of view stronger than the author's? Once you have thought about these questions, present a clear and easy-to-follow thesis. Here is a critique outline:

1. Introduce a topic.
2. Give your main idea or theme in a nutshell.
3. Give background on the work.
4. Who do you think is the audience this work was intended for?
5. Describe the key people, locations, and plot.
6. Give your estimates of the strengths and what you liked.
7. Talk about what you liked or didn't like.
8. Tell why you liked or disliked some points.
9. Would you recommend the book? Why (or why not)?

Back up your thesis with well-thought-out arguments, and wrap it up with a succinct conclusion. Your critique will then represent a strong stand regarding the materials. It will have plenty of substance and be something you're proud to submit.

1

86   *STUDENT SUCCESS SECRETS*

A Guide for Evaluating Literature

Literary Characteristic	Example	Description/ Evaluation	Remarks
Clarity of style	Works by Ernest Hemingway	Simple language, vivid description.	Classic style.
	Works by John Steinbeck	Clear language, depiction of real life experiences, believable and real characters.	Often depressing themes.
	Works by Ayn Rand	Logical thought, uses comparisons of people as they are to people as they should be.	Idealistic and often pollyanna endings.
	Works by Fyodor Dostoevsky	Well-defined true-to-life characters, straight-line type development of characters.	Characters almost become stereotyped.
Lack of Clarity	Works by James Joyce	Stream of consciousness style of writing, uses flashbacks, flash-forwards, element of unreality.	Story line is often bewildering and hard to follow. Relationships between events difficult to determine.
	Works by Edward Albee	Uses symbolism dealing with author's innermost feelings, as typified by the play, **Tiny Alice.**	Difficult to understand, hard to relate to author's experiences because of symbolic plot structure.
Realism	Works by Fyodor Dostoevsky	Complicated plots dealing with real people, true-to-life situations, and believable events, as typified by the novel **Crime and Punishment.**	

FIGURE 10-2

A Guide for Evaluating Literature *(continued)*

Literary Characteristic	Example	Description/ Evaluation	Remarks
Surrealism	Works by Anthony Burgess	Use of extremes and shock to develop satirical themes, as typified by the novel **A Clockwork Orange.**	Language is virtually a foreign language. Must understand author's purpose in order to understand plot and theme.
Escapism	Works by Ian Fleming	Use of mystery and suspense. Themes tend to avoid serious life problems. Characters are heroic, larger than life.	Typified by James Bond stories.
	Works by J.R.R. Tolkien	Use of fantasy. Reality is suspended.	Fables—almost an Alice in Wonderland quality.
Theme of morality	Contrast **War and Peace** by Tolstoy with **Barabbas** by Lagerkvist	Moral conflicts. Hero is faced with a decision of what is morally right.	Often depressing yet important conflicts.
Political Themes	Contrast **The Memoirs of Richard Nixon** with books written by John Dean, H.R. Haldeman, and John Ehrlichman	Political writings.	Note how diifferent authors treat the same historical event.
Religious	Contrast **Angels** by Billy Graham with **The Faith of a Rationalist** by Bertrand Russell	Theological writings. Develop extensive background in both Eastern and Western theology.	Watch how each builds his case for or against theology.

FIGURE 10-2

A Guide for Evaluating Literature *(continued)*

Literary Characteristic	Example	Description/ Evaluation	Remarks
Themes of philosophy	Contrast **The Communist Manifesto** by Karl Marx with **Atlas Shrugged** by Ayn Rand	Contrast extremes.	Books with philosophical themes reflect opposites in the author's ideology.
Artistic Detail	Works by Tennessee Williams	Economy of words approaches poetry. Creation of character is based on creating empathy, as typified in the character of Blanche in the play **A Streetcar Named Desire**.	Note usage of language, color and symbolism.
	Works by Thomas Wolfe	Use of nostalgic description, as typified by **Look Homeward Angel.**	

FIGURE 10-2

Review These Points

Prepare for It
Meet the Author
Organize the Information
Prime the Mind
Sharpen Your Questions
Develop a Point of View

11
WRITING MADE EASIER:
Nonfiction and Fiction

WRITING NONFICTION

Some students do not like to write. This is usually because of several things—they may have had a bad experience when doing it before, no one ever taught them an easy way to do it, or they may not be familiar with how easy it is to do it on a computer. Writing can be very satisfying and, with some practice, you can learn to get it done fairly quickly. In this chapter, you'll learn how to do two types of writing: the nonfiction research-type writing and free-expression fiction. Remember, while this chapter has many useful ideas and strategies, it will take some practice, so be ready!

For many students, writing a long paper is tough. But you might not have been taught how to research and write a paper. This section shows you, step-by step, how to produce the best paper you are capable of writing. You'll learn how to make your paper organized, how to make it flow and how to present your material for maximum results.

Research Papers Start with an Idea

You need a starting point of ideas. You'll either be assigned a topic or get to choose one on your own. In either case, you'll want to do some preliminary exploring. You can sort through your own textbook or notes to find a topic, or you can go to the library and do some exploratory research. You might open up your computer and browse the Internet for some ideas. To get the real data, the solid background needed for a good paper, you'll want to use some of the research tools available. There's plenty!

Sources of Research Information

- On-line databases available through search engines to specific web sites
- Newsearch, a database from over 3,000 publications
- Newsletters (consult Newsletters In Print)
- CD-ROMs that can be borrowed from or used in media centers
- Clipping services that locate news articles or key words
- Transcripts of TV shows obtained from their listed 800-number
- *World Book, Collier's,* or *Encyclopedia Britannica*
- Specialized encyclopedias (like *Afro-American Encyclopedia, The New Jewish Encyclopedia, New Catholic Encyclopedia, Encyclopedia of World Mythology,* and *New International Wildlife Encyclopedia*)
- Public libraries; public interlibrary reference loans
- Interlibrary computer connections

- Your friends, relatives, parents, and community members
- University and college libraries
- Specialized libraries within the university
- Historical society libraries
- Museum or exhibit libraries
- Research center libraries
- Magazine articles (use the *Readers' Guide to Periodical Literature*)
- Newsmedia sources; send for videos from TV
- Newspaper articles (use your library's database)
- Business Dateline (collects business news)
- *Facts on File* or *The New York Times On-line Database*
- Almanacs—*The World Almanac and Book of Facts* and *Time Almanac: with Information Please*
- Yearbooks—*The Statesman's Yearbook: Statistical and Historical Annual of the States of the World, Chase's Calendar of Events, Washington Information Directory*
- Dictionaries (today's dictionaries offer more than definitions)
- Who's Who publications, such as *Who's Who in America*
- U. S. government bulletins and freebies

Pick a topic that appeals to you, one that you're interested in learning about. Once you've picked a possible topic, do a bit of follow-up to determine whether or not it's the right one for you. To get general information about a topic, read an authoritative article on the subject, such as one in an encyclopedia. Does the topic still seem interesting to you? Can you tell if it's going to be too narrow or too broad? Does it have some controversy to it? Timeliness? A sufficient number of other sources? Only after you have answered these questions can you make an informed and accurate decision about your final topic.

Shape Your Topic

After you have made your initial decision about the topic, you'll want to take it to the next level of development. Now you'll need a point of view for your paper. Think about a thesis, an argument, a direction for the topic. As an example, doing a paper on the growth of the civil rights movement in America would be a major undertaking. However, if you focused on the key role of President Lyndon Johnson or the role of the media, you'd have a narrower topic and a possible point of view. The next step in shaping your ideas is to begin a rough outline. But include only main or key ideas in this preliminary outline. Start with your topic in the center and make branches coming out of it like the spokes of a wheel. Put different areas you want to talk about on different branches. Then you can actually see how many subtopics you have and how much information you can expect to generate for each of them. Soon you'll have an idea of how much you have to work with and what else you need to learn.

Gather Your Sources

The best place to make your first run on information is the library. Talk to a staff member and ask for suggestions. Look up your topic in the card catalog or computer catalog. Check a general index to magazine articles, such as the *Readers' Guide to Periodical Literature*, or appropriate specialized indexes, such as *The Humanities Index* or *The New York Times Index*. Do an on-line bibliographic computer search for your topic, if your library has this service. Use other reference books, such as encyclopedias and bibliographic publications that are available for many subjects, to locate what might be important sources. Depending on your topic, you might find that the pamphlet or map sections have useful information for you.

Again, a great source for getting information about your subject is the reference librarian. Do not hesitate to ask for suggestions and directions at any point in your search. The librarian also will be able to give you basic general guidance about how to use the library.

The preliminary bibliography you prepare will serve you in many ways. First, it's great to find out early in your project if you have adequate information for the research you need to do. Second, by collecting your sources early, you can process requests for interlibrary loans, if necessary. And third, the information you gather may further shape or refine your original title.

Be sure to use the most recent publications so that your research provides the reader with the advantage of the most accurate and up-to-date information. Collect more sources than you think you'll need; many of the sources may not turn out to be as useful as you thought they would be, plus, some of the sources may suggest others. If you're using your computer, open up a file and name it "Sources." If you're not, list each source on a separate 3" × 5" index card. Include author, title, publisher, date and place of publication, edition, card catalog number, pages used, and your comments about the appropriateness of the source (for example, core source, borderline source).

Sort Your Information

Now you're ready to begin gathering pertinent data from your sources. Start with the easiest and most general sources first. Look for basic information on your topic, then scan it. Begin to build your subject knowledge, and start making a mental note of names and places that appear several times. Gain more and more background on the topic, moving from source to source. Mark your source index cards with a notation to reference any especially key source. On the back of each 3" × 5" card, put any key ideas from the material. That way, you'll only need to look up a source once, unless it's one of the few that you decide to study in depth later. If you're using your computer, make sure you put all your key information under each heading so you won't need to go back later to organize it. In general, try to spend only a few minutes on each source, before moving on to the next.

Get Your Material Organized

Now that you've narrowed the topic, located relevant sources, and gained background on the subject, you're ready to begin a structural formulation. This means you need to begin to see your paper's skeleton before you start fleshing out your writing. Your paper will have several predictable sections.

- **Introduction.** Grab the reader's interest with an unusual story. Introduce the topic to the reader— its scope, width, and direction. State the importance, timeliness, and impact of the topic. Tell why you chose the topic. Summarize your thesis in a clear, concise statement. Motivate or tantalize the reader to read on.

- **Background.** Give a brief history of the topic. Be interesting. Briefly introduce other areas of your topic. Help the reader know what you know—key points only. Explain any terminology, key words, or phrases.

- **Main Body.** State strongly and truthfully your thesis and viewpoint. Use accurate, strong, unemotional language. Present arguments and ideas in easy-to-agree order—from least to most controversial, from strongest to weakest in reasoning.

- **Counter-Argument and Rebuttal.** State any opposing viewpoints. Assess their strengths and weaknesses. Build a case to further reinforce.

- **Conclusion.** Restate your thesis and your reasons for believing in it. Briefly walk the reader through your arguments and ideas. Analyze and evaluate your key points for the reader. Introduce no new information; restate prior ideas clearly. Conclude with a succinct and moving statement.

Before you begin writing, organize the main topics and subtopics into a list on your computer. It might look like this:

Introduction
- grab interest
- introduce topic
- state importance
- say why topic was chosen
- summarize thesis

This pre-outline will start your mind thinking about how to fill in the blanks and avoid writer's block. It's a great brain prompter.

Write the Rough Draft

You have the first two key ingredients to begin writing—the background notes and the structural framework. How do you know how much to write on each section of the paper? One thing that may help you is to make some guesses about the final length you want your paper to be. Then start assigning approximate page lengths to each part.

- Introduction................5–10%
- Background 10–20%
- Body..........................40–60%
- Rebuttal......................5–15%
- Conclusion..................5–10%

Following this apportionment, on a twenty-page paper your introduction might be two pages, background three

pages, body twelve pages, rebuttal two pages, and conclusion one page. This is only a guideline. Your teacher
may have different standards. Check what the expectations are *before* you begin writing your rough draft.

The easiest way to write, by far, is to use a computer.
If you don't have one, many libraries have them, and full-
service copy shops can rent one to you. You may also
have a friend with one who can show you how to use it.

Now is the time to start writing. But instead of starting at the beginning, start on any part of the paper. Why?
It's more important to get the ideas and words flowing.
Start with simple statements and don't worry about how
it sounds—not yet. Just start writing! You can edit your
work later. You might start with the section on background of the topic. The introduction is much easier to
write *after* you have done most of the paper. Also, the
background gets you grounded and refamiliarized with
the material. The material then becomes easy to discuss

and easy to organize. It also then becomes easy to say a lot about the material. After the background section is complete, move on to the main body of the paper. Write as long as you can, then take a short break. As soon as you can, while you're fresh, go right back to it again.

Keep the stream of thoughts coming, and write as long as you're producing good material. If you get stuck, take a longer break and come back when you're rejuvenated. There's no rule to follow about writing papers—just write as long as it's working. Some students can write well into the night and others do best in the morning, from about nine until noon. Just write when you're at your best and keep going until it's done, then get away from it for a while. You'll have a fresh perspective when you come back to it.

Edit and Proofread

After you have taken a break from your material, go back and read it aloud. It should read well, as if you were hearing a speech on your topic. Put in transition phrases where necessary. Make sure all the spelling is correct. Check for errors in logic and flaws in statistical data. Have another set of eyes go over the paper, such as a friend's, in order to get feedback. Add stronger words (use a thesaurus) to increase the clarity or impact. Consult a handbook on style and usage to be sure that you have used the proper format for your paper and that your grammar is correct.

Documentation

Documentation is critical to your success. An excellent resource for this process is *10 Steps in Writing the*

Research Paper, *6th edition* by Roberta and Peter Markman and Marie Waddell (Barron's Educational Series, 2001). Make sure you have given credit where it is due, that you have either inserted quotation marks or set off any quoted material, and that you have given correct and complete references for your sources.

Double check to be sure you have avoided plagiarism. Plagiarism is where you lift, take, copy, or otherwise steal someone's phrases, sentences, or paragraphs without giving credit to them. Never cut and paste what others have written, even on the Internet. You wouldn't steal money and you shouldn't steal writing, either. If you like what someone said, that's fine. Just remember that you might be able to say it better or update it. If it's too good to change, and you just use a couple of words or sentences, simply put quotes around it. Then make sure you identify the author. Being a good writer does not mean that you never use the thinking and writing of other people. It means that when you do it, you do it in appropriate ways. As my wife, Diane, always said to me, "You'd be surprised how flattered other writers are when they are mentioned in your books. Just make sure you give them credit."

The bibliography is always the last section of the paper. Use the bibliography cards you made when you began your research. The three most common types of entries you will need to know are:

1. **Books**

   Jensen, Eric. *B's and A's in 30 Days*. Hauppauge, New York: Barron's Educational Series, Inc., 1997.

2. **Articles, Reports**

   Bills, R.E. "The Effect of a Value on Learning," *Journal of Personality 21* (1952): 217 22.

3. **Other Sources**

   DePorter, Bobbi, with Mark Reardon. Discussion at Learning Forum Offices, Oceanside, California, May 16, 1995.

Final Polish

Unless otherwise specified by your instructor, print out your work double-spaced, with one-inch margins on each side. Make sure that you number all the pages. Put your paper into something to protect it (like a file folder) and include a title page. Center the title and put your name under it. Also include the date, name of course and instructor, and any special designations your class may have.

Your final copy is expected to be printed on regular white bond paper. Make sure your paper is perfect in its presentation—no smudges, stray marks, or errors. The neatness of your paper does affect the grading, whether it's a conscious decision by the instructor or not. Be meticulous and rigorous in assessing the quality of your paper before you turn it in (on time!). If you follow all of these steps carefully, you'll have a good shot at getting an A.

WRITING FICTION

Many times you'll be expected to write creatively. While it's a bit challenging at the start, you may be surprised to know that there are some pretty good formulas

---

Seven-Step Fiction Process

1. **Idea generation.** Use tools like clustering and fastwrites.

2. **First draft.** Get your rough ideas stated and expanded.

3. **Feedback.** Read your writing to someone and get your first feedback.

4. **Rework.** Take the feedback and implement what's relevant. This is your second draft.

5. **Editing.** Now get serious about the structure, grammar, and spelling.

6. **Feedback.** Read this once again, getting feedback on your changes.

7. **Fine tuning.** Take the feedback and implement what's relevant. Prepare the paper for presentation.

---

for making the process easier. The steps you'll be learning can be used with most types of fiction. This includes short stories, poetry, drama, novels, and almost any other form of creative expression.

Idea Generation

One of the biggest complaints you'll hear from writers is: "I can't seem to get started. I just don't have any ideas." There are many good ways to stimulate your natural creativity. Let's explore two of them—clustering and fastwrites.

Clustering is a simple concept that requires only blank paper and a pen or pencil. Let's say the topic you've been assigned to write about is *Change*. Write the word change in the center of your piece of paper and circle it. Now just do uncensored, free word association.

That means, no judgments or opinions, just let your mind run wild. Every word you can think of that change reminds you of, write it down in areas around the center. It might look a little like this:

Pocket Full of Change

Changes in Lattitude

Temporary and Permanent

Change

Resistance to Change

Change Can Be Good

Change for the Better

Fear of Change

Change of State Change My Mind

Local and Global Changes in Motion

FIGURE 11-1

As you can tell, this process generated a lot of ideas. Now, go back to your paper and cross out any of the associations that were on the wrong track. Once you have those eliminated, use the remaining words to do more free associations. Then, go back and cross out any that took you off track. Now go back again and do more brainstorming. In a short time, you have many ideas to write about. There's a moment when you'll get so excited about your ideas (or tired of brainstorming) that you'll want to start writing. But there's an intermediate step.

Once you have a topic, with good subtopics, simply number the ideas in order of how you might write about them. You could number them based on importance, based on the flow of the writing, or based on what you know about them. After they're numbered, you can begin to put some ideas on paper or in the computer.

There's another technique for generating ideas and concepts; it's called *fastwriting*. This concept is simple: Set a timed goal and simply write no matter what. Start with a goal like five minutes. You'll need paper and pen or a computer in front of you. When you start, write any and every thought that comes to mind, on or off your topic. Forget grammar, sentence composition, syntax, vocabulary, spelling, flow, or anything—just write!

If you can't think of anything to write during this five-minute time slot, simply write, "I'm not thinking of anything at this moment." If you get bored or tired, write, "I'm bored and tired." The point is, you'll only tap into your brain's best creativity when you stop saying "I can't do it" and start doing it. What will this do for you? It will unleash many ideas, some of which may be exactly what you need to get started.

First Draft

Now that you have some ideas, from either clustering or fastwriting, put something down. Get your rough ideas stated and expanded so that you've at least got a starting point. Stay relaxed and loose during this process; your writing is just in the early stages.

First Feedback

Each of us lives in our own world. It's often said that writers live in the loneliest world of all—their own mind. At this early stage, it's critical to get some feedback from someone. The best way is simple. Ask a friend, a parent, a teacher, or, perhaps as a last resort, your brother or sister, to be an audience. Tell them what kind of feedback you want. Tell them what to listen for. Read it out loud to them. Don't expect them to jump up and cheer for you, they probably won't. But at least they can say things like, "It was really emotional" or "I was lost most of the time."

Rework the First Draft

Nobody, not even the most famous or best writers, get it 100 percent perfect the first time. You won't either, and that's OK. Take the feedback and implement what's relevant. If the listener was confused or lost, make it clearer. If it was clear but it had no impact, consider that you may need to do much more *sensory writing*.

As an example:

Nonsensory writing might go like this: "I was so hungry, you wouldn't believe it. So, after hours of waiting for something, we arrived at the spot for dinner. Unfortunately, the place was packed and my patience was short. This made for some major frustration on my part."

As you go back and reread that last paragraph, notice how the writer of the paragraph didn't tell the reader (you) much about what he or she saw, heard, felt, thought, smelled or tasted. In fact, you have to just guess about all of those. This style of writing (nonsensory) makes writing boring and, even more important, fails to communicate much at all to the reader. *Sensory writing* is different. The same paragraph might be rewritten to sound like this:

As an example:

"My stomach had that kind of hollow aching hunger that hurts from deep inside. Even my head felt off-balance, kind of tilted. Everything I saw, the red billboards, the busy stores, and well-fed people, all reminded me of food. In a sick way, I wondered what it was like for prisoners in a concentration camp. Time slowed to a crawl. I told myself, 'Just a little longer; you can make it.' When we finally arrived at the single-story Italian diner, dozens of people were shouting, pushing, shoving, elbow to elbow, each crowding closer to the overwhelmed hostess. Each was hoping for a miracle to push their sacred reservation closer to the top of her illegible three-page list."

Quite a difference, isn't it? In the first, nonsensory, paragraph, it was up to the reader to make up most of the understanding. In the second, the sensory writing paragraph, the reader had a better idea of what was going on. That's what you want to do—use *sensory-rich* language. It makes all the difference between whether you simply tell the reader what's happening or you provide a real multi-media presentation.

Editing

Now is the time to get serious about the structure, grammar, and spelling. The two best ways to fix this are to read it out loud, and to check the resources. You'll read it out loud because you want your writing to sound the way people really talk. It should sound smooth, not choppy or chunky. This gives you a great sense of what it will sound like for the reader who reads it. The other form of editing is to use resources. That means a spell-check on a computer. It could mean using a book or Internet resource that has stylistic guidelines to fine-tune the flow. Using a search engine, type in "MLA style sheet" for help.

Second Feedback

By now, your work is taking shape; you've got most of the bugs worked out. It's starting to make good solid sense. But once again, you are in need of feedback. Read this again, out loud, to another person. You need their feedback on your main draft. This time, read it with passion. Read it with emphasis. Read it in a way that moves people. You've put your soul into this work, now let it shine! Then, pause, relax, take a deep breath, and listen to their feedback.

Fine-tuning

Take the feedback without any judgment and thank the person. You shouldn't try to persuade the other person that their impressions were wrong—it was just their gut reaction. In fact, if you have to explain the ideas of your work, it tells you that it needs more work. The ideas should be self-explanatory. If someone else can't figure it out, maybe no one will. After listening, decide if you agree or disagree with the feedback. Then, implement what's relevant.

Prepare the Paper for Presentation

Now it's time for the window dressing. Get the paper printed up neat and clean. Put a title on it. Make sure your name is on it. Make sure the page numbers are on every page. Double check for any missing pages, missing words, or flaws—you can often do this right on the computer. Do a spell-check and print out a rough draft to proof one last time. Make sure all quoted phrases have the quotation marks on each side. Does it look great? If so, it's ready to turn in!

Review These Points

Writing Nonfiction
Research Papers Start with an Idea
Sources of Research Information
Shape Your Topic
Gather Your Sources
Sort Your Information
Get Your Material Organized
Write the Rough Draft
Edit and Proofread
Documentation
Final Polish

Writing Fiction
Idea Generation
First Draft
First Feedback
Rework the First Draft
Editing
Second Feedback
Fine-tuning
Prepare the Paper for Presentation

12
TEST-TAKING:
Making It Easier

Schools are expensive to run. It costs, on the average, about $5,000 a year (that's up to twelfth grade; double that figure for a university student), per student to make it happen. Add up the number of students in your school and you can see it gets quite expensive. So, to make sure the money is being well spent, many want to find out if schools are doing what they are supposed to be doing. Is learning and achievement really going on? How much? While we all wish that our learning was the one and only thing parents, teachers, and administrators cared about, it's not. Schools want to find out if you can prove that you are learning. That, in a nutshell, is the brief theory of testing. While you may be most interested in your learning, you end up having to play the academic game at school called test-taking.

We all know that in life, there's the ideal situation and there's the reality. Let's start with the ideal and you can come as close to it as you possibly can. An effective study program that will help ensure success is one that is planned from the beginning of the course and carried on, step by step, throughout the school term. So, here it is, the best possible case scenario.

THE FIRST FEW WEEKS OF CLASSES

To score high on tests, start the first week of school. Find out about your teacher's basic requirements for the course. Is student creativity encouraged or is the class run by the rules? What kind of classwork is expected? What are the standards for excellence? How important are textbooks? Can you use the Internet for research or ideas? Exactly what should your homework look like? Can you ask questions? Can you talk with your teacher after class? Should you schedule a meeting if you're lost? Are there tests from last year that are available for study from the teacher? All of this information will help you steer your learning in the direction of what the course and teacher boundaries are. It's silly to gain real knowledge and skill in a topic and still fail a course, simply because it was on the wrong topic or packaged wrong.

How else can you prepare ahead of time? There are many things you can do. Should you do all of them? Ideally, yes. In reality, do as many as you can, whenever you think of them. What works is to think of your class, and school in general, as simply a way to learn the skills and knowledge you need to learn for life. No matter what subjects you learn in school, in life you'll still need many things: a positive and persistent character, basic understanding of how things work, learning skills, people skills, emotional skills, teamwork practice, goal-setting, and confidence. Meanwhile, here's what you can do during the term:

- Browse ahead in your texts.
- Make sure you have a study buddy or learning partner lined up.

– Figure out some of the main ideas that will be coming up.

– Stay up-to-date with your daily To Do list.

– Take notes from your textbook before you go to class; it saves time and increases your understanding. As you read, ask yourself questions or bring them to class.

– Add class lecture notes to your home text notes; always trying to consolidate and unify them.

THE MIDDLE OF THE COURSE

Should you study every day? Research suggests that you should do something every day, even if it's for only five minutes. It's a lot more effective and less stressful than cramming.

Ask questions often in class. Do it when you don't understand course material; don't put off your questions or you will forget about them. Once you ask a question, feel free to write down the information. Often, the confidence or enthusiasm of the moment means we often fail to follow-up on our notes as we should.

Sit in the first three rows in class. You can see better, you can hear better, and it shows an interest on your part. Make sure your posture is good, too. If you sit back and look bored (even if you are), teachers receive a negative impression of you. Sit up and lean forward.

See your teacher for help early in the term, not the day before a test. This will show a genuine interest on your part, and the extra contact may pay off later if you need extra help. Be sure to introduce yourself, give your name, and let the teacher know what you liked or didn't like about the class. Most teachers appreciate tactful and honest input. It can help make the class more interesting to you, as well as helping you to learn better.

Browse through your class background material. The more you read about a topic, the greater your understanding, and the faster you will be able to read it. Gaining a wide background in a subject area will give you a big edge at test time. Put the concept in five words or less (rhymes are even better) on one side of a 3" × 5" card. Use these flashcards to review key concepts. You should keep reviewing your notes to make sure you can recall them anytime you want.

THE LAST WEEK BEFORE THE TEST

Find out what kind of exam will be given and alter your studying accordingly. If an objective test is scheduled, use more memory techniques and concentrate on details. For a subjective one, many say the best approach is to get a wide background in that subject, stressing ideas rather than details. Concentrate on knowing something about almost everything. You can do that with the use of flashcards or making the memory maps, as in the notetaking chapter (Chapter 6).

Rework your notes into a new format, trying to see the material from new angles. Review sessions are helpful, but get together with others only if they are good students. Otherwise, you may be really "soaked" for information, and learn nothing yourself. A C student usually doesn't help an honor roll student, so study with the best students you can find.

THE LAST FEW DAYS BEFORE THE TEST

At this point, start identifying what you don't know. Many students review by going over material they already know well. Often, parts they don't know are ignored, making their study process ineffective. Don't pat yourself on the back for what you *do* know, find out what you *don't* know. How do you find out what you know and don't know?

– Check your notes. Cover up a part of them and ask yourself what's there.

– Use flashcards to test your knowledge.

– Use the index of your textbooks. If you're studying Chapters 1 through 5, figure out what page numbers that covers. Let's say it's pages 1 to 100. Go to the index, and start with the first entry you see with a number between 1 and 100. Ask yourself if you understand that term, and continue until you come across an unfamiliar term. Look it up in the text, read about it, then take notes on it so you won't forget again. This system allows you to check yourself on every term, idea, person, and detail in the entire textbook.

– Turn to the end of your text chapters and review a summary.

– Check for a listing of the author's questions. This can be helpful in directing your study efforts.

– At many colleges and universities, tests used during previous terms are kept on file in the library.

These can be a gold mine because many teachers don't rewrite a test each term. Often, the tests used may just be scrambled questions from old tests.

A positive attitude is crucial the few days just before an exam. The upcoming test is not an execution; it is just a chance to show what you have learned. Your teachers want you to get good grades because it reflects on their teaching success. Many regret students doing poorly because that reflects their failure to communicate important concepts.

Look at the exam as a challenge and an opportunity to show what you have learned. Admit to yourself that you probably won't know every question; that way, you won't get discouraged when you see a test question you can't answer. Tests are necessary in most subjects, as they're about the only way the teacher knows you know the material.

THE HOURS BEFORE THE EXAM

You have already finished the hardest part of the race. If you have kept up during the term, you have already "passed" the exam. The last minutes may be the difference between an A and a B. Others may have exam fever, but you can relax a bit. Get a full night's sleep and be sure to get some exercise the day of the exam. That encourages better blood circulation, hence a better supply of oxygen to your brain during exam time. You will be able to think more clearly. Of course, it is best to exercise in moderation so that you are invigorated rather than exhausted. A brisk walk before the test is a good way to get exercise.

STOP AND TAKE ACTION

◆ The morning of your test, eat protein for breakfast (that's a good idea every day). Protein is synthesized into amines that boost alertness and sharper mental performance.

◆ Eat good foods, but eat lightly or not at all within an hour of your test. If you do eat, your body's energy and blood supply will be drawn toward your stomach for digestion instead of toward your brain where it is needed during test time.

◆ Be sure to review all notes and texts.

◆ Browse through each chapter, making certain to expose your mind to as much information as possible. If you have kept up, all will be a review, and cramming won't be necessary. Your confidence and calm mental attitude will encourage recall at the time of the exam.

◆ A review the night before the exam should take only two to three hours.

◆ On the day of the exam, arrive five to ten minutes early to your class.

◆ The best way to relax is to prepare mentally.

◆ Get the seat you want in class and practice recalling.

EXAM TIME

Now you can cash in your efforts. First, read the entire exam thoroughly. By seeing questions in advance, you will give your subconscious mind time to come up with answers. Second, allot your time wisely. Note which questions are given the most point value and which are the most difficult. Don't pick up your pen for a few minutes. Stop to think about your attack plan.

Be relaxed and calm while you plan your approach. A good test taker doesn't fight tests; the secret is to relax. Interpret and rephrase questions several ways to be sure you understand them. Then, start with the easiest problems first, and work quickly and neatly. Structure and organize before you answer because neatness does count, regardless of what an instructor will say. Be sure to keep in mind the test directions as you answer. Don't overread questions by assuming they are more complex than they seemed at first glance. Read them for what you believe is the intent of the question. Notice critical or key words in each question such as *show*, *contrast*, *define*, and other similar directions. Try to answer every question unless you absolutely have no idea of the answer; wrong answers are often subtracted from right ones.

SPECIFIC TEST FORMATS

Schools are changing the way they assess students, so you'll be getting very different types of tests. In general, these tests provide a healthier approach to finding out what's being learned. The new types of testing will include more uses of videos, journals, models, projects, writing, interviews, plays, music, audio- and videotapes, computer work, and community work. These will give you a better range of options to discover not only *what* you know but, more important, *how* you know it. The key thing for you is to ask, ask, and ask. Find out what the teacher expects and what you need to do differently.

For the older types of test, the more objective ones, you'll have several formats. They include questions in a true-false, multiple-choice, matching, or fill-in format. Usually the answer is provided but the student must decide among several possibilities. Here are some guidelines:

True-False Questions

True-false questions are the easiest test questions for the obvious reason that you have at least a fifty-fifty chance of getting the right answer. First, be sure you have read the question correctly. Look for words such as *always* or *never*; these words often indicate a false answer. Words such as *often, usually, rarely,* or *sometimes* can indicate a true answer. Decide if the statement is totally true before you mark it true.

Also, be sure to answer what the tester intended, not what you read into the question. For example, the statement, "General Motors produces compact cars," is true. If the question had read, "General Motors *alone* produces compact cars," then it would be false. On true-false questions, stick with your first impression. Studies have shown over and over that your first impression is usually right, so be slow to change your answer, if at all.

Multiple-Choice Questions

When answering multiple-choice questions, remember to read the answers first. This way, you'll view each answer separately and equally, without "jumping" on the first and easiest one. Look for an answer that not only seems right on its own, but completes the question smoothly. If the question asks why something occurs, then your answer must be a cause. Try to eliminate any obviously poor answers. Suspect as a possible right answer phrases such as *all of the above, none of the above,* or *two of the above.*

Check the wording of questions to notice qualifying phrases such as "all of the following are true *except* . . ." or "which two of the below are *not* . . ." Statistically, the least likely correct answer on a multiple-choice question is the first choice. When in doubt, pick the longer of the two answers. But, just as in true-false sections, always put something down. Traditionally, students would back up a few problems and say, "Well, I haven't had a *B* selection for a while; I'll just put that down." Chances are that there is not a mathematical model used for random selection of answers. It makes more sense to intuit the answer from the applicable question. Even a guesstimate is better than a random choice or leaving it blank and getting it wrong for sure.

Sentence Completion or Fill-in Questions

These generally ask for an exact word from memory. They don't allow for much error, so make sure your answer is a logical part of the sentence as a whole. Use the length and number of blanks that are given as a hint. Make sure the grammar is consistent. When in doubt, guess. Even if it's a generalized guess, you may get partial credit. If you are unsure of two possibilities, include both and hope for half credit.

Essay Tests

When answering questions on an essay test, begin by making an outline on a piece of scrap paper. Assemble and organize the main points. Check the wording of the question to make sure you are interpreting it correctly. For example, if the question asks you to compare and contrast, do not give a description or a discussion. Begin your essay by using the same words that are in the question. Keep your answer to the point.

Always write something in answer to a question, even if you don't have much to say. Think and write by using this format:

1. **Introduction**—Introduce your topic.

2. **Background**—Give historical or philosophical background data to orient the reader to the topic.

3. **Thesis and Arguments**—State the main points, including causes and effects, methods used, dates, places, results.

4. **Conclusion**—Include the significance of each event and finish up with a summary.

When totally stumped for an answer on an essay, think about book titles, famous names, places, dates, wars, economics, and politics. Usually something will trigger some ideas. If you know nothing about the essay question, invent your own question on the subject and answer it. You'll usually get at least partial credit. That's better than nothing.

THE AFTERMATH

Is your test over when you finish the last question? Not even close! Three important steps remain that can make the difference between a lower and a higher grade: Q & A, name, and filling in. You'll need to act quickly to get these steps done, so start right in and move fast.

First, Q & A (questions and answers) means you'll reread as many of the earlier questions as you can and reread all of your answers. Make sure you read the question correctly, without reading too much or too little into it. Rework anything that needs fixing. Eliminating careless errors can save some disappointment later and raise your score.

Second, your name is equally important. Be sure you've written your name in clear, visible letters. This is also the time to benefit from earlier positive encounters with your teacher. Any positive impact you've made earlier might now pay off. Sometimes a good impression can give you a higher grade in a borderline situation.

Finally, when you think you've finished, turn the test over and sit with it for a moment. Many times tests are turned in too fast and a student thinks of something to say *after* it's too late. Just let your mind wander a moment. If you have the time, you might daydream and think about your test for up to five minutes. Every now and then, something really good will pop into your head, now that the pressure's down a bit.

Once your corrected test is returned, look it over. Check your errors and find out not *what* they were, but what *kind* of errors they were. Was it from answering questions too quickly, poor organization, a missed assignment, or incorrect notes? Understand why you made errors and avoid the problem on the next test.

Review These Points

The First Few Weeks of Classes
The Middle of the Course
The Last Week Before the Test
The Last Few Days Before the Test
The Hours Before the Exam
Exam Time
Specific Test Formats
True-False Questions
Multiple-Choice Questions
Sentence Completion or Fill-in Questions
Essay Tests
The Aftermath

13

THE 1 PERCENT
SECRET

Is there a simple or easy formula for success in school? If there were one, it would have been packaged and sold at your local supermarket a long time ago. Maybe someday scientists will invent memory pills or speed-reading potions. For now, the closest we will all get to a miracle solution is the 1 percent solution. What is this secret?

The answer makes sense when you think about your brain. The sensory receptors in your brain seem to be the most sophisticated ever found in nature or man-made. Through our eyes, we process about 100 million bits of data per second. In fact, the most frequent decision we make is where to shift our eyes for attention (over 100,000 times per day). From our ears to our brains, we receive about 30,000 bits per second. The rest of our body, like our hands, feet, and all of our skin receptors, sends a stream of data that can exceed 10 million bits per second. In short, our brain is processing an enormous amount of sensory input, and it relays very little of it to our conscious attention.

Why don't you find out about all these noises, sights, and sensations coming into your body? Probably, because if you were aware of it all, you'd be over-whelmed with useless information. Your brain is an unlimited processing storehouse of forgotten data,

dreams, nightmares, commercials, skills, books, voices, and suggestions. And because it has the accumulations of a lifetime, much of its stored information is out-of-date. So, although your brain has a nearly limitless capacity, it is not designed to always act in your best interest. As an example, one might buy a product that is bad simply because that company advertised it more than one that is good. The tobacco companies have built an empire on this concept.

What does all this have to do with the 1 percent secret? Simple. You are aware of only 1 percent of all the information that comes across your mind on a daily basis. And, while you can't control the other 99 percent, you can influence the 1 percent in some key ways. How? You can't change every habit all at once. But you can make small changes, every day. Like 1 percent. That's right. By just making small, realistic, and practical changes of just 1 percent a day, over time, you'll make all the changes you could ask for. A small change, multiplied by all the other small changes, carried out on a daily basis, is very powerful.

The best type of small changes, you can make on an everyday basis, are in either *skills* or *attitude*. For either of those, you'll want some simple reminders. A reminder can be a simple statement, a slogan, or key words that keep you on track for the long term.

What follows are called affirmations. Years ago, the conventional wisdom was that these were more on the fringe or, at worst, a bunch of baloney. However, the power of suggestion has gained increasing acceptance by mainstream medicine and neuroscience. You'll find examples in Dr. Larry Dossey's *Healing Words* and

Dr. Norman Cousins' *The Anatomy of an Illness.* The power of prayer, placebos, affirmation, and suggestion have finally gotten the credit they are due. In fact, the Food and Drug Administration insists that all new medicines be tested against a placebo to be sure they are, in fact, actually doing what is claimed. Why? Placebos have a success rate of 30 to 80 percent, depending on the application! No wonder more and more of them are used.

Your school success affirmations are provided for you in the following pages. You may choose to use them or pass on them. You may copy them onto another piece of paper, one that's more colorful, then post them up. Or, you can simply flip through these pages every day as a way of embedding the ideas in your mind for the long term. In either case, use them with confidence. They certainly can't hurt, and you may be pleasantly surprised.

DIRECTIONS FOR ATTAINING YOUR GOALS

Use your 1 percent solution often because the more often you advertise these positive thoughts to your mind, the faster you'll reach your goals. Practice at least once a day, although additional practice is always more helpful. Here are some good times to practice: Upon awakening in the morning, during a boring TV show, before a nap, and before you fall asleep at night. That's when the brain is most receptive, according to Harvard psychiatrist Dr. Allan Hobson.

The process is incredibly simple and rewarding. You can change old patterns without effort or sacrifice. Each time you read your goal statements, something positive happens. You are making a definite step toward your goal because every thought will register. Stay positive; the results are rarely immediate.

As long as you continue to use your 1 percent reminders, you are breaking down old objections and resistance. The positive suggestions will then become stronger than the old habits and you will begin to act successfully. It will be comfortable and natural. You may be amazed to realize that, where once you objected to your new goals, they now seem so normal. You will have established a new habit pattern, improved your confidence and self-image, and, of course, your school habits. More important, you'll affirm and be forever aware that you are in control of your life. Your life will happen by your design and not by chance; therefore, if you design it well, you can have the life you want.

Simple enough, isn't it? It's a small price to pay for the benefits of being successful; yet, this is the challenge for everyone, the challenge of change. Change is not always easy, but it can happen. And it's exciting. The feeling of success comes from knowing you're on the right path. There's nothing like it. Because if you have that feeling, the feeling that self-programming and positive thinking can give to you, then you'll be a success in anything—not just in school, but in relationships, athletics, business, and life.

Let's say you are inspired to get started. You already have some goals for yourself. Or, at least, you have some ideas. Ideas can be powerful. Every time you think a thought, you strengthen neural pathways in your brain. If you think of failing often enough, your brain will already have that habit. The more you think of succeeding, the more likely you'll succeed. To help build powerful habits of success, refer to this book daily. Both the strategies and the following affirmations can and will make a difference. They will create strong, lasting neural pathways. Over time, you'll have a permanent beneficial effect. That's a promise!

GOALS FOR SUCCESS

GOAL 1 **STUDY SKILLS**

Suggested Affirmations

I can learn to enjoy studying. I can learn to look forward to studying every day. I have plenty of time to study and find every subject interesting. I am enthusiastic and excited about studying. I always browse through textbooks before reading them. I observe the style, organization, and vocabulary. I prepare each section before reading. I can learn to gather main ideas quickly and easily. I can learn to read my texts with excellent comprehension. I review each chapter quickly and thoroughly. My notes are getting better every day.

Suggested Daily Actions

◆ Plan your study work for the day.
◆ Browse through your textbooks before studying them.
◆ Gather main ideas and take creative notes.

GOAL 2 GREAT READING SKILLS

Suggested Affirmations

I love to read and I try to find plenty of time for reading. I read quickly and effortlessly. I read in large word groups, absorbing difficult material without hesitation. My comprehension is excellent, as is my memory.

Suggested Daily Actions

◆ Ask questions before, during, and after reading.
◆ Scan quickly for key ideas.
◆ Put your key ideas into creative notes.

GOAL 3 **IMPROVED NOTETAKING**

Suggested Affirmations

I enjoy taking notes and find them easy to do well. My notes represent the material clearly and creatively. I use my own shorthand and vary the size and shape of headings. I know the basic formats of most subjects and use them when designing my notes.

Suggested Daily Actions

◆ Use a set of colored pens.
◆ Use large sheets of unlined paper.
◆ Experiment with pictures, illustrations, and symbols.

GOAL 4 — IMPROVED MEMORY

Suggested Affirmations

My memory is better and I enjoy remembering information. I retain my material with ease and completeness. My memory is improving and I am more aware each day. Whatever information I need comes to me instantly and easily through perfect recall.

Suggested Daily Actions

◆ Use more motor and contextual/spatial memory.
◆ Develop rhymes and key word systems; and use acronyms.
◆ Remember things several ways—by sight, sound, and touch.

GOAL 5 ► INCREASING VOCABULARY

Suggested Affirmations

I have an ever-increasing vocabulary and enjoy learning new words. I read new and unusual materials, thus adding new words daily. I have flashcards and I practice them daily. I associate with people who have an excellent vocabulary in order to learn new words. I use the dictionary to increase my vocabulary. I notice how new words are spelled and check for the word roots. I enjoy an excellent vocabulary and use it daily.

Suggested Daily Actions

◆ For today, learn one new word.
◆ Stay in the habit of looking up new words.
◆ Use new words once you've learned them.

GOAL 6 ▶ BETTER TEST-TAKING

Suggested Affirmations

I look forward to taking tests and enjoy the opportunity to show what I know. I prepare myself thoroughly for each test. I review all class lecture notes, textbook notes, and related data. I easily memorize all pertinent information. I am confident and relaxed at exam time. I first preview the test, then plan my strategy. I move quickly and effortlessly through the exam. Correct answers instantly come to mind. My answers are clear and true. I am a successful test-taker.

Suggested Daily Actions

- ◆ Learn or study something every day.
- ◆ Ask plenty of questions in class.
- ◆ Bring confidence and over-preparation into tests.

GOAL 7 ▶ CONCENTRATION

Suggested Affirmations

I am able to concentrate with ease. I block out distractions quickly and automatically. I focus my mind on the task at hand and complete it accurately. Other noises that I hear are normal everyday sounds, that flow with my thinking and increase my concentration.

Suggested Daily Actions

◆ Get rid of all distractions before studying.
◆ Set short-term goals.
◆ Provide fresh air and water.

GOAL 8 ▶ **BETTER HEALTH**

Suggested Affirmations

I enjoy perfect health. I am energetic, enthusiastic, and outgoing. I enjoy small portions of health-giving, wholesome foods. I experience an abundance of energy, vibrancy, and youth. My body functions perfectly. I am alert, healthy, and strong. I keep my body in perfect condition and exercise daily. I enjoy exercising and my body is becoming firmer, stronger, and full of vitality. I think only thoughts of health, energy, and life.

Suggested Daily Actions

◆ Eat protein, fruit, and vegetables every day.
◆ Give your body a workout at least three times a week.
◆ Save your carbohydrates for later in the day.

GOAL 9 ▶ ENJOY LEARNING

Suggested Affirmations

I enjoy my classes and look forward to attending them daily. I thirst for knowledge. I satisfy my need for knowledge by attending all my classes and consulting my instructor. I find school challenging, rewarding, and positive. I meet interesting people at school and form satisfying relationships. I have an intense desire to become a success, and school is the key for me.

Suggested Daily Actions

◆ Today, learn something for fun.
◆ Learn something in each class for yourself.
◆ Share or celebrate something you've learned.

GOAL 10 ▶ THINKING POSITIVELY

Suggested Affirmations

I enjoy positive thoughts. I am a grateful person who has learned to appreciate my health, my family, conveniences, friends, and opportunities. I look for the good in others. I practice the golden rule, knowing that a smile is powerful. I feel comfortable with others and find compliments easy to give. I allow others to be who they are, and give them understanding and warmth.

Suggested Daily Actions

- ◆ Take in everything today with a smile.
- ◆ Whatever happens that is bad, find something good in it.
- ◆ Think a positive thought about someone you don't like.

GOAL **11** ▶ **INCREASED CONFIDENCE**

Suggested Affirmations

I am an important person in my world. I am on the path to being successful. I am an intelligent, free-willed being with the power to choose. I am talented, capable, and honest. I am warm, sincere, worthy, and creative. I like myself more each day. I have a tremendous and unlimited potential. I am learning to love myself and appreciate my talents and abilities. I am unique and rare. I am valuable and rich in thought. I am an expression of love, happiness, and confidence. I believe in myself and my future. I am calm, relaxed, and confident in any situation. I control my destiny. I am free.

Suggested Daily Actions

◆ Do something for yourself today.
◆ Give yourself a new challenge to try.
◆ Notice how well you do things today.

GOAL 12 ▶ PUTTING IT ALL TOGETHER

Suggested Affirmations

Today, this new day, I am a successful student. Overnight, my mind and body have produced thousands of new cells to give me the greatest possible advantages. I am born anew, revitalized, and full of energy. I am rare and valuable, unique in all the universe. I have unlimited potential. I believe in my abilities, attitudes, and goals. I get only one shot at life, so today I push myself to my limits. I use the skills and knowledge from this book every day. I begin and end the day with a success. My goals are being reached every day and I seek them eagerly. I act positively and happily, fully accepting myself and others. I live to the fullest by experiencing life without limits. I embrace life.

I approach each class, each book, and each assignment with enthusiasm, happiness, and joy. I thirst for knowledge. I eat well, knowing the importance of fruits, vegetables, protein, and grains. I look forward to reading and believing this reminder each and every day. I work out every day because I can only do in life what my health and vitality will allow me to do. I am a positive and successful student. I know each step I take is part of a longer journey on the path of success. I am clear on my goals and see myself, hear myself, and feel the energy of myself reaching my goals. I now begin to realize my greater potential, and my burden lightens. I

241

smile and laugh. I realize that I have planted the seeds for lifelong success.

Suggested Daily Actions

◆ Use one idea from this book today.
◆ Notice something you did well today.
◆ Appreciate something in your life today.

EPILOGUE

You read this book because you wanted to have more tools to succeed in school and life. But, surprisingly, your greatest fear is not that you won't succeed. Your greatest fear is that you now have all the tools to succeed already. After all, if you have everything you need now, what's left to hold you back? What possible excuses could you use? It's scary, isn't it?

By now, you've realized that you can become anything you want. Everyone is motivated by different things, and I hope you've found the right motivation for yourself. Actually, reading this book shows you've already motivated yourself pretty well. You've learned many valuable tools in this book—the knowledge of an excellent study procedure; how to read better, take more effective notes, improve your vocabulary, and improve your memory; techniques for evaluating fiction; how to write papers; and secrets to taking tests. You've learned that you can do anything you set your mind to doing, and what an important tool that is! So, now that you've finished this book, put what you've learned to use. You know you deserve success, so go for it!

BIBLIOGRAPHY
AND SUGGESTED
READING

Bromberg, Murray, and Melvin Gordon. *1100 Words You Need to Know*, 4th ed. Hauppauge, NY: Barron's Educational Series, Inc., 2000.

Carnevale, Linda. *Hot Words for the SAT: The 350 Words You Need to Know*. Hauppauge, NY: Barron's Educational Series, Inc., 2001.

Bromley, Karen, Linda Irwin-deVitis, and Marcia Modlo. *Graphic Organizers*. New York: Scholastic Professional Books, 1995.

Buzan, Tony. *The Mind Map Book*. New York: Plume Publishing, 1996.

———. *Speed Reading*, 3rd ed. New York: E. P. Dutton, 1991.

———. *Use Both Sides of Your Brain*, 3rd ed. New York: E. P. Dutton, 1991.

———. *Use Your Perfect Memory*, 3rd ed. New York: E. P. Dutton, 1991.

Carper, Jean. *Your Miracle Brain*. New York: HarperCollins, 2000.

Cousins, Norman. *An Anatomy of an Illness*. New York: Bantam Doubleday Dell, 1991.

DePorter, Bobbi, and Mike Hernacki. *Quantum Learning*. New York: Dell Paperbacks, 1992.

Dossey, Larry. *Healing Words: The Power of Prayer and the Practice of Medicine*. San Francisco: HarperSanFrancisco, 1995.

Gawain, Shakti. *Creative Visualization: Use the Power of Your Imagination to Create What You Want in Your Life*, 25th ed. Novato, CA: New World Library, 2002.

Howard, Pierce. *Owner's Manual for the Brain*. Austin, TX: Bard Press, 2000.

Hutchison, Michael. *Mega Brain Power*. New York: Hyperion Press, 1994.

Jensen, Eric. *Brain-Based Learning.* San Diego, CA: The Brain Store, 2000.

———. *B's and A's in 30 Days.* Hauppauge, NY: Barron's Educational Series, Inc., 1997.

———. *Learning Smarter.* San Diego, CA: The Brain Store, 2000.

Kline, Peter. *The Everyday Genius.* Arlington, VA: Great Ocean Publishers, 1988.

Kline, Peter, and Martel Laurence. *School Success.* Arlington, VA: Great Ocean Publishers, 1994.

Lofland, Don. *Powerlearning.* Stamford, CT: Longmeadow Press, 1994.

Markman, Roberta H., Peter T. Markman, and Maria L. Waddell. *Ten Steps in Writing the Research Paper,* 6th ed. Hauppauge, NY: Barron's Educational Series, Inc., 2001.

Markowitz, Karen and Eric Jensen. *The Great Memory Book.* San Diego, CA: The Brain Store, 1999.

McCarthy, Michael. *Mastering the Information Age.* New York: Jeremy P. Tarcher, Inc., 1991.

Miles, Elizabeth. *Tune Your Brain.* New York: Berkeley Books, 1997.

Ornstein, Robert. *The Healing Brain.* Malor Books, 1999.

———. *The Psychology of Consciousness,* New York: Harcourt Brace Jovanovich, 1977.

Porter, Patrick. *Awaken the Genius.* Phoenix, Arizona: Awaken the Genius Foundation, 1994.

Rose, Colin, and Malcolm J. Nicholl. *Accelerated Learning for the 21st Century.* New York: Dell Pub. Co., 1998.

Schnaubelt, Kurt. *Advanced Aromatherapy: The Science of Essential Oil Therapy.* Rochester, VT: Inner Traditions Intl Ltd, 1998.

Scheele, Paul. *The PhotoReading Whole Mind System.* Wayzata, Minnesota: Learning Strategies Corporation, 2000.

Strunk, William Jr., E. B. White, and Roger Angell. *The Elements of Style,* 4th ed. Boston: Allyn & Bacon, 2000.

NOTES